World

ls

noirs

r mixed voices

iled and edited by
Bob Chilcott
Susan Knight

MUSIC DEPARTMENT

OXFORD

OXFORD
UNIVERSITY PRESS

Great Clarendon Street, Oxford OX2 6DP, England
198 Madison Avenue, New York, NY10016, USA

Oxford University Press is a department of the University of Oxford.
It furthers the University's aim of excellence in research, scholarship,
and education by publishing worldwide in

Oxford   New York

Auckland   Bangkok   Buenos Aires   Cape Town   Chennai
Dar es Salaam   Delhi   Hong Kong   Istanbul   Karachi   Kolkata
Kuala Lumpur   Madrid   Melbourne   Mexico City   Mumbai   Nairobi
São Paulo   Shanghai   Taipei   Tokyo   Toronto

Oxford is a registered trade mark of Oxford University Press
in the UK and in certain other countries

PREFACE

World Carols for Choirs brings together 31 new carols and carol arrangements by composers from all over Europe, the Americas, Africa, Asia, and Australasia. In keeping with the ever-widening global context in which so many of us live, this collection attempts to embrace the choral traditions of cultures worldwide.

The composers we asked to provide carols for this project include both established writers and writers whose work may be new to many. In some instances, the composers have chosen to arrange a traditional carol from their own cultures. Some of the sound-worlds of these carols will be more traditionally familiar to English-speaking or western European choirs, as with the lovely old melodies arranged by Eleanor Daley from Canada, Vic Nees from Belgium, and the German Karsten Gundermann.

Other carols draw us into less traditional sound-worlds, from Selga Mence's bell-like version of a Latvian carol and Vahram Sargysan's powerful and large-scale arrangement of an old Armenian chant, to Tony Guzmán's infectious dancing version of Ramón Díaz's dynamic song. Other composers have chosen to create completely new carols with new words and music. These include the Australian Stephen Leek's *Southern Cross*, which gives us a feel of Christmas in the sunshine, and Carl Rütti's *Im Silbernen Wassergrund*, in which the Swiss composer brings to life the dense text with his hallmark bitter-sweet harmony. *Infant Joy* by the Japanese composer Rikuya Terashima uses the well-known William Blake poem—not strictly a Christmas piece, but one that tells eloquently of the joy of new birth.

All the carols here have been published in the original language, but each one also includes a singing translation in English—most of which have been prepared especially for this collection. For those who feel inspired to sing the carols in the original language, we have provided pronunciation guides written for each piece by the composers and other experts. Alternatively, we hope that the translations will offer a singable option.

What is clear to us is that each piece brings its own sound- and musical world to tell the story of the birth of Jesus. We hope that the collection will help to refresh the repertoire of choirs all over the world, at a time when singing together brings us closer together.

Acknowledgements

We would like to thank the BBC Singers along with Michael Emery and Stephen Ashley-King for their marvellous singing on the recording associated with this collection. Thank you also to Jeremy Jackman and Tim Morris for their translations of the texts, and to the following people (in addition to the composers) for their assistance in preparing or editing the pronunciation guides: Ildiko Allen, Åse Bergstrom, Arthur Bobikyan, Hermann Eckel, Tomasz Habraszewski, Oliver Kuusik, Pippa Mayfield, Anna Kirsten Nygaard, Irena Rozman, Nicole Tibbels, Henry Vermaak, Lilija Zobens and staff at the Iceland Music Information Centre. Special thanks go to David Blackwell and Jane Griffiths for their work on this volume, and to Kristen Thorner for all the marvellous work she has done to bring it to life.

Bob Chilcott and Susan Knight
June 2005

CONTENTS

INDEX

INTRODUCTION

1. Argentina
Eduardo Falú, *Villancico de la Falta de Fe (For a World Without Faith)*

The composer and guitarist Eduardo Falú (b. 1928) is one of Argentina's most celebrated musicians. He has toured and performed throughout North and South America and across Europe and has a prodigious output of compositions, many of which have been recorded. Eduardo Falú has received honorary doctorates from the Universidad Nacional de Río Cuarto and the Instituto Universitario Aeronáutico de la República, and he is a member of the Argentinian National Academy of Music.

The *villancico* is a popular form of religious song developed in Spain in the fifteenth century and later adopted in Latin America. *Villancicos* are traditionally sung by children on Christmas Eve, but they are also sung by adults, drawn by their deep mystical meaning and sincerity. A characteristic of the Latin American *villancico* is a focus on the material needs of the newborn child, which include instruments so that he may dance. Like many traditional *villancicos*, *Villancico de la Falta de Fe* has a simple syllabic melody with gentle cross-rhythms; in this case, the accompanying voices seem to imitate the sound of a guitar.

2. Armenia
Movses Khorenatsi arr. Vahram Sargsyan, *Khorurd Metz (Great Mystery)*

A graduate of the Yerevan Komitas State Conservatory (2003), where he studied with Ashot Zohrabyan, Vahram Sargsyan (b. 1981) is a composer principally of choral works. He is also active as a choral conductor in Armenia, and his music has been performed across Europe, and in North America at the Sixth World Symposium of Choral Music in Minneapolis (2002).

Khorurd Metz is an Armenian sacred hymn for the feast of the Nativity. This form of hymn, or *sharakan*, was the principal genre of Armenian sacred music between the fifth and fifteenth centuries. Movses Khorenatsi, who wrote both the words and the melody, was one of the Armenia's greatest *sharakan* composers, and his melody persists throughout this modal, polyphonic arrangement, passing from one voice to another. Vahram Sargsyan's style is influenced by the choral music of Komitas Vardapet (1869–1935), one of the founders of the Armenian national school of musical composition.

3. Australia
Stephen Leek, *Southern Cross*

The Australian composer and conductor Stephen Leek (b. 1959) has been active at the forefront of developments in choral music in Australia since the early 1980s. His music captures the energies, rhythms, and colours of his homeland and is performed across the globe. For over a decade Stephen Leek has worked collaboratively with librettist Elizabeth Anne Williams, who is herself an acclaimed choral conductor and educator. He has received numerous awards, including the prestigious Robert Edler International Choral Prize (2003), and with his choir, The Australian Voices, he promotes the music of Australian composers around the world.

On the oldest and smallest continent on the planet, the star formation of the Southern Cross is an important physical and symbolic icon for survival and encapsulates a national pride. The five stars have traditionally assisted sailors in navigating their way to Australia, and on the land have been beacons leading the way across the vast open Australian spaces. In this cheerful work the Southern Cross is likened to the Star of the East that led the Wise Men to Bethlehem.

4. Basque Country, Spain
Javier Busto, *Kuttun Kantak* (*Night Songs*)

Javier Busto (b. 1949) graduated in medicine from Valladolid University. Trained in choral conducting by Erwin List, he has conducted many choirs including the Eskifaia Choir in Hondarribia (1978–94) and Kanta Cantemus Korua in Gipuzkoa (from 1994), both of which he founded. He is internationally known as a composer of sacred choral music and his scores have been published in the Basque Country, Germany, Sweden, the UK, and the US.

In the Basque Country Christmas carols are traditionally sung in the streets and country lanes. The carols have a unique character, combining the directness of peasant expression, the more refined musical style of the church, and the natural rhythms of the language. Basque carols embody the universal sentiments of nostalgia, sadness, warmth, and happiness, and they still enjoy enthusiastic support today. *Kuttun Kantak* consists of three songs: a lullaby with characteristic cross-rhythms; a prayer in irregular metre; and a song of rejoicing.

5. Belgium
Trad. arr. Vic Nees, *Nu is die roe van Jesse* (*The Rod of Jesse*)

A native of Mechelen (Malines), Belgium, Vic Nees (b. 1936) studied composition with Flor Peeters in Antwerp and choral conducting with Kurt Thomas in Hamburg. In 1961 he became a producer of choral music for Flemish Radio in Brussels. He conducted the Radio Chorus from 1970 to 1996 and is a member of the Belgian Royal Academy. Among his numerous choral compositions, the Magnificat has been performed in many countries.

Like the art of the 'primitive' Flemish painters, most Flemish carols of the sixteenth century depict the Christmas story in simple local imagery. This particular song was composed somewhat later, at the time of Rubens, and already uses more theological imagery. It was first published as a bicinium (duo) in 1651 in Bruges. In Vic Nees's arrangement the harmonization becomes richer with each successive verse, culminating in six-part harmony in verse 4.

6. Brazil
Ernani Aguiar, *Acalanto para o Menino Jesus* (*Carol for the Baby Jesus*)

The composer, conductor, and teacher Ernani Aguiar (b. 1950) is one of the most active musicians in Brazil. He studied in Germany and Italy as well as with eminent musicians in his native country before becoming a professor at the Federal University of Rio de Janeiro. His instrumental and choral compositions have enjoyed wide international success. Aguiar is a fellow of the Villa Lobos Institute and a member of the Brazilian Academy of Music.

Brazil is a huge country and embraces many diverse Christmas customs. Songs, dances, and particular traditions surround the practice of singing Christmas carols. Among the most notable are *pastorinhas* (which are traditionally sung around the manger on Christmas Eve and represent the shepherds' visit to Jesus) and *lapinhas* (Christmas night pageants featuring the baby Jesus). In these events sung music has great importance, and the texts are colloquial, using the local dialect of the people celebrating. *Acalanto para o Menino Jesus* was written for the feast of the Conception of the Virgin Mary and illustrates the Italian influence on Brazilian culture.

7. Canada
Trad. arr. Eleanor Daley, *The Huron Carol*

Eleanor Daley (b. 1955) is an organist and pianist but is probably best known as a prolific choral composer with a gift for melody and for the sensitive setting of text. While she also writes and arranges secular music, she regularly composes sacred choral music for her church choirs in Toronto, and her music has been published and performed throughout the US, Europe, South Africa, and the Far East. Both her compositions and her recordings of them have won national awards in Canada.

The original version of this carol is the earliest-known Canadian Christmas carol. It dates from about 1643 and was composed by the French Jesuit missionary and linguist Father St Jean de Brebeuf (1583–1649). Father Brebeuf was stationed at Sainte-Marie Among the Hurons, where he served the Huron people. Written originally in the Huron language, the carol was then known as *Jesus Ahatonhia* and was based on a sixteenth-century French Canadian melody. It is now widely known and sung throughout Canada. Eleanor Daley's arrangement presents each of the verses in a different setting while preserving the modal flavour.

8. Canada (Quebec)
Trad. arr. Gilbert Patenaude, *Notre divin Maître (Our master, Lord Jesus)*

Gilbert Patenaude (b. 1947) is a native of Quebec and studied composition at the Conservatoire de Montréal. He is best known as a choral director, notably of Les Petits Chanteurs de Mont-Royal, which he founded in 1978, and of the music department of the College of St Laurent. A prolific composer, Patenaude is famous throughout French Canada for his choral music, operas, songs, and instrumental works.

The traditional carol *Notre divin Maître* comes from a collection known as *Noëls Anciens de la Nouvelle-France* (Ancient Carols of New France). The melody derives from an old drinking song but has been associated in Canada (principally in Quebec) with a religious Christmas text since the middle of the eighteenth century.

9. Dominican Republic
Ramón Díaz arr. Juan Tony Guzmán, *¡Llega la Navidad! (Christmas is Coming)*

A native of the Dominican Republic, Juan Tony Guzmán (b. 1959) has conducted choirs, bands, and orchestras in the US, Canada, Europe, and Central and South America. His works include both original compositions and arrangements of Caribbean and Latin-American music. As a teacher he specializes in music education and jazz; he is also a professional engineer.

¡Llega la Navidad! is a *villancico*, or Christmas carol (see notes on Argentina), in the style of the *merengue*, the Dominican national dance. This carol expresses the rejoicing of the Christmas season with a simple melodic and harmonic structure and characteristic folk rhythms. It is accompanied by percussion instruments popular in Dominican culture.

10. Estonia
Trad. arr. Mart Siimer, *Nüüd ole, Jeesus, kiidetud (Now blessed be thou, Christ Jesu)*

Born in Tallinn, Mart Siimer (b. 1967) graduated from the Tallinn Conservatory in 1990 as a student of Eino Tamberg, and later studied at the Eastman School of Music in Rochester, USA. His compositions include chamber music, orchestral pieces, and numerous choral works, some of which have been performed by mass choirs at Estonian festivals. An organist, pianist, and teacher of composition, Mart Siimer has also worked as music critic for several Estonian newspapers.

Estonia was one of the first regions of Europe to join the Reformation of the sixteenth century and to adopt the hymns of the Lutheran Church. This carol belongs to the genre of folk variations on Lutheran hymns: the original hymn, with a text mostly by Luther, is *Gelobet seist du, Jesu Christ*. After being translated into Estonian, the text eventually became separated from the melody and gave rise to new tunes. This particular tune comes from the island of Kihnu off south-west Estonia, where folk tradition is exceptionally well preserved: indeed, some inhabitants still wear traditional costumes in everyday life. In verse 3 the composer has added a contrasting section, following an Estonian tradition. The accompaniment may be adapted for organ and/or other instruments.

11. Finland
Pekka Juhani Hannikainen arr. Pekka Kostiainen, *Tuikkikaa, oi joulun tähtöset* (*Twinkle bright, you stars of Christmastide*)

Pekka Kostiainen (b. 1944) graduated from the Sibelius Academy, Helsinki, in both church music and composition. A lecturer in music at the University of Jyväskylä (from 1971), he is also the founder and conductor of the Musica choir at the university and director of the children's choir Vox Aurea. His considerable choral output has been widely distributed and performed both in Finland and abroad.

Tuikkikaa, oi joulun tähtöset is one of the most popular of all Finnish Christmas carols. Its text was written by Elsa Koponen, a teacher, who remarked on how eagerly her young pupils sang the Christmas songs, their eyes shining as brightly as the stars in the sky. This joy is tinged with sadness in the mournfully beautiful melody, composed for this text by Pekka Juhani Hannikainen (published in 1918), and in Kostiainen's somewhat nostalgic harmonization.

12. France
Bruno Gousset, *Ainsi que parmi la prée* (*On a hillside in the cold*)

A Parisian musicologist and pianist, Bruno Gousset (b. 1958) currently works as an opera coach and as an accompanist for amateur and professional choirs. He is a self-taught composer, and his output includes operas, symphonic works, chamber and piano music, songs, and cantatas for chorus and orchestra.

This carol is an original composition on a text in Old French which skilfully summarizes the story of the Nativity in rhyming verse. The composer's use throughout of a hypnotic, rhythmic melody alternating with long, sustained notes captures perfectly the pastoral and mystical essence of the text.

13. Germany
Trad. arr. Karsten Gundermann, *Süßer die Glocken nie klingen* (*Sweetly the Bells are Ringing*)

Karsten Gundermann (b. 1966) is a native of Dresden, where he pursued graduate studies in composition at the Dresden College of Music. He undertook further graduate work in opera composition at the National Academy of Chinese Theatre Arts in Beijing, and composition studies in theatre and film music at New York University, before becoming a freelance composer in Hamburg.

This carol describes how the ringing of church bells evokes the events of the first Christmas. Although some people find it a little mawkish, it is still sung in Germany, mostly by the older generation. The melody comes from another German folksong, *Seht wie die Sonn dort sinket* (1826), and the text was written by Friedrich Wilhelm Kitzinger (1816–1890). Karsten Gundermann's arrangement uses the lower voices to evoke the sound of bells.

14. Ghana
Robert M. Kwami, *Krismas ɖodzi vɔ* (*Christmas Time is Here*)

Robert Mawuena Kwami (1954–2004) was a professor of music at the University of Pretoria in South Africa and director of the Centre for Intercultural Music Arts in London. His extensive experience included teaching and lecturing in educational institutions in both African and European countries. Highly regarded by his musical and academic colleagues worldwide, he left over 30 compositions and 70 publications; his untimely death was profoundly lamented.

Krismas ɖodzi vɔ is in the Ewe language of eastern Ghana. The text invites us to listen to the angels who are proclaiming the birth of Jesus Christ. The angels' song itself, using words from the Bible, draws on Ghanaian 'highlife', a popular dance style dating from the early twentieth century. The performers may move or dance joyfully during this section.

15. Hungary
Trad. arr. Miklós Kocsár, *Nagykarácsony Éjszakáján* (*On Great Christmas Night*)

Miklós Kocsár (b. 1933) is a composer principally of vocal and chamber music, whose style is rooted in the Bartókian tradition. He studied composition with Ferenc Farkas at the Liszt Academy of Music (1954–59) and from 1963 worked as musical director and conductor of the Madách Theatre in Budapest. He was Head of Composition at the Budapest Conservatory between 1974 and 1984 and in 1974 joined Hungarian Radio, serving as head of the music section in 1984–85. He has been awarded many prizes, including the Erkel Prize (1973, 1980), the title of Artist of Merit (1987), the Bartók-Pásztory Prize (1992), and the Kossuth Prize (2000).

Nagykarácsony Éjszakáján draws on traditional sources. The first three verses are set to one of Hungary's most treasured melodies, while the remaining verses incorporate two immensely popular Hungarian Christmas tunes as found in István Volly's collection.

16. Iceland
Þorkell Sigurbjörnsson, *Immanúel oss í nátt* (*Emmanuel, to us this night*)

Þorkell Sigurbjörnsson (b. 1938) began his musical studies at the Reykjavik School of Music but completed his undergraduate and graduate degrees in the US. He is active as a teacher, pianist, lecturer, conductor, radio commentator, and organizer of musical events, in addition to being one of Iceland's best-known composers. He has written over 300 works (many of which have been recorded), including 25 hymns or arrangements in the Icelandic Hymnal. Þorkell Sigurbjörnsson is a member of the Royal Swedish Academy of Music.

The original carol *Immanúel oss i nátt* comes from the manuscript *Hymnodia Sacra*, a collection of songs made by Pastor Gudmundur Högnason of the Westman Islands, Iceland, in 1742. Högnason is thought to be the author of the texts and many of the melodies, including that for *Immanúel oss i nátt*. Þorkell Sigurbjörnsson's arrangement is in the Dorian mode and adopts the bar-form of many Luthern chorales. The piece meditates on the birth of Christ with harmonies of increasing richness before ending with echoes of the opening motif.

17. Ireland
Séamas de Barra, *Carúl Fáilte* (*A Carol of Welcome*)

Séamas de Barra (b. 1955), a native of Cork in southern Ireland, is best known as a composer of choral music. He studied composition under Aloys Fleischmann and has twice been commissioned by the Cork International Choral Festival. In 1993 he was asked to write a new work for the 500th anniversary of Christ Church Cathedral in Dublin. His music has been performed by the King's Singers, the BBC Singers, and many Irish choirs, most notably the Irish Youth Choir, for whom he wrote *Canticum in Laudibus* (1988) and *Overture to a Masque* (2002). Some of his shorter choral pieces—including the *Gloria* and *Magnificat*—have recently been recorded by the Cork-based chamber choir Madrigal '75.

This carol was specially commissioned for inclusion in this collection. The text, written by the composer, attempts to capture something of the emotional immediacy and directness of expression characteristic of Irish devotional folk poetry.

18. Japan
Rikuya Terashima, *Infant Joy*

Rikuya Terashima (b. 1964) studied composition at undergraduate and graduate levels at the Tokyo National University of Fine Arts and Music. He has performed and collaborated with many leading artists as composer and pianist in concerts, theatrical productions, and recordings. His major works include operas, chamber music, and pieces for Japanese traditional instruments.

Since Japan has no tradition of carol composition and few poems suitable for setting as carols, Terashima has set a text from William Blake's *Songs of Innocence*. The composer regards the themes in the text of joy, mercy, pity, peace, and love as particularly relevant in a carol setting because of their universal appeal. Most of the carol is based on the pentatonic scale, which reflects the sense of innocence in Blake's poem.

19. Korea
Hyun Chul Lee, *Jajang, jajang, Ahgi Yesu* (Lullay, lullay, Baby Jesu)

Born in Korea, Hyun Chul Lee (b. 1973) studied composition in the US at Georgia State University and under Stephen Young at the Westminster Choir College of Rider University in New Jersey. A specialist in children's music, he has worked as composer-in-residence to the Worldvision Korea Children's Choir (under the conductor Hee Churl Kim) with which he has participated in numerous children's choral festivals around the world.

The main melody of *Jajang, jajang, Ahgi Yesu* is a popular Korean lullaby which has been handed down through many generations. In the carol Mary, mother of Jesus, is depicted singing her child to sleep; the lilting style of the outer sections contrasts with the more declamatory passage starting at bar 26.

20. Latvia
Trad. arr. Selga Mence, *Dedziet skalu, pūtiet guni* (Bring us fire, bring us light)

Selga Mence (b. 1953) was born in Liepaja, Latvia, and specialized in composition at the Latvian Academy of Music, Riga; she later became associate professor of composition there. In addition to composing orchestral and chamber music, she has written many choral works, which have been performed throughout Latvia and in other European countries, particularly at international choral festivals.

Dedziet skalu, pūtiet guni comes from the rich repertoire of folksongs used to celebrate the winter solstice in Latvia, an ancient tradition dating back to before the arrival of Christianity. Given that long history, it is interesting that it was only in 1960 that the composer Vilnis Salaks collected this melody and text in the Dagda region of the country; this bespeaks volumes for the power of folk transmission. Selga Mence's arrangement presents the two phrases of the original song in a variety of textures, beginning and ending with imitations of the sound of bells.

21. New Zealand
David Hamilton, *Lullaby Carol*

David Hamilton (b. 1955) was head of music at Epsom Girls' Grammar School, New Zealand, until 2001. He is deputy musical director of the Auckland Choral Society and has been composer-in-residence to the Auckland Philharmonia. He concentrates on composing while maintaining a part-time involvement in music education and is well known as a choral conductor and workshop leader. His choral music has been widely performed and has been published in the UK, US, and Finland.

Lullaby Carol was written for a church choir and has a fifteenth-century English carol text. Its musical style reflects the English choral tradition in its use of modal harmonies which give the piece a slightly archaic quality. English choral music came to New Zealand in the nineteenth century and still underpins much choral work in the country. The carol alternates a lullaby refrain with a starker, more declamatory style setting references to Jesus' crucifixion.

22. Nigeria
Christian Onyeji, *Amuworo ayi otu nwa* (*For unto us a child is born*)

Christian Onyeji (b. 1967) is a Nigerian composer, pianist, choreographer, conductor/music director, and theatre director. He has a Doctor of Music degree from the University of Pretoria, South Africa, and is currently a senior lecturer at the Department of Music, University of Nigeria, Nsukka Enugu State. He is a researcher on African music and a composer of modern African art music, whose works have been widely performed both locally and internationally.

Setting text from Isaiah 9: 6, *Amuworo ayi otu nwa* is a piece for church worship in the style of modern Nigerian art music. The music draws on elements of rhythm, dance, polyrhythm, and texture from Nigerian choral music deriving from the Igbo sub-area. Such compositions—commonly known as 'Native Airs'—are popular with Nigerian art music lovers. *Amuworo ayi otu nwa* has been performed several times in its original form by the St Paul's Anglican Cathedral Choir, Nsukka, Enugu State, Nigeria, and by other choirs during Christmas services.

23. Norway
Ola Gjeilo, *Det hev ei rose sprunge* (*A spotless rose*)

Ola Gjeilo (b. 1978) studied the piano and organ in his native Norway. Although he is also jazz-trained, since 1999 he has focused on writing classical music. He has studied at the Norwegian Academy of Music, Oslo; the Juilliard School of Music, New York (with Robert Beaser); and the Royal College of Music in London. As a composer he has focused on chamber and choral music. His works have been published in Norway and the UK, and performed and recorded by such leading choirs as the Oslo Chamber Choir, the Oslo Philharmonic Choir, and the World Youth Choir.

Det hev ei rose sprunge has had a long life in Norway, where it was first known with a German melody and text. It was translated into Norwegian by Peter Hognestad in 1919–21 and has become one of the most popular carols in Norway. Ola Gjeilo has chosen to give the old text new life in this freshly composed, highly sonorous setting.

24. Poland
Trad. arr. Stanisław Szczyciński, *Hej, hey, lelija!* (*Hey, hey, lily*)

Born in Warsaw (1954), Stanisław Szczyciński studied both music and mathematics. As a composer he concentrates on song, but he has also written and arranged film music and many choral pieces. He is also a pianist who enjoys playing popular music, ballads, and jazz, and a singer in groups specializing in early music.

Hej, hej, lelija! is a traditional folk carol, collected in the nineteenth century by the famous Polish folklorist Oskar Kolberg. The text describes the tender mothering of the newborn Jesus by the Virgin Mary, for whom the Polish people have a special devotion.

25. Slovenia
Trad. arr. Maksimiljan Feguš, *Ena noč polna veselja* (*On a starlit night*)

The Maribor composer Maksimiljan Feguš (b. 1948) studied composition and conducting at the Academy of Music in Ljubljana. He was for a number of years chorus master of the Slovene National Opera, Maribor, and later became a senior lecturer in composition and theory at the music department of the University of Maribor's faculty of eduction. His compositions include symphonic music, works for voices and instruments, incidental music for the stage, and chamber, solo, and choral pieces. They have been frequently performed throughout Slovenia and increasingly across Europe.

Ena noč polna veselja is an arrangement of a traditional *kolednica* (Christmas carol) from Kamnik and Braslovč. It is the first in a series of four carols entitled *Štiri Slovenske Ljudske Božične* (*Four Traditional Slovene Christmas Carols*), composed in 1999.

26. South Africa
Peter Louis van Dijk, *Susa ninna*

Born in Rotterdam in the Netherlands, Peter van Dijk (b. 1953) settled in South Africa, where he has worked extensively as an orchestral and choral conductor and a teacher. As a composer he is internationally known for his operas, ballets, and choral works with orchestra. His music has been published in Germany, the UK, and the US, and has been performed and recorded across southern Africa and in Egypt, Europe, New Zealand, and North America.

Susa ninna was inspired by, though is otherwise unrelated to, the Middle Dutch poem 'Genekat ons den Avenstar' ('The Evening Star is near'), written *c*.1350. The carol was commissioned by the Foundation for the Creative Arts (SA), specifically as a composition in Afrikaans. It was first performed in Johannesburg City Hall in December 1993 by the South African Broadcasting Corporation Choir and the National Symphony Orchestra of South Africa. Although the carol begins and ends as a soothing lullaby, the second verse reaches an exciting climax which expresses the celebration of Christ's birth.

27. Sweden
Robert Sund, *Ett Nyfött Barn* (*A Newborn Child*)

Although he graduated from Uppsala University in social sciences, Robert Sund (b. 1942) soon turned to music full-time as a singer, conductor, and composer. After conducting studies with Eric Ericson at the Royal College of Music in Stockholm, he began a successful conducting and teaching career. Active as a conductor in Sweden and abroad, he was named Conductor of the Year in Sweden in 1993, and his choir, Orphei Drängar, was Swedish Choir of the Year in 2003. He is well known for his choral and instrumental compositions and arrangements.

The text of *Ett Nyfött Barn* was written by Christer Åsberg, formerly general secretary of the Swedish Bible Commission. In his musical setting Robert Sund has tried to match its simple style and expressive character, which seem to evoke the innocence of the newborn child.

28. Switzerland
Carl Rütti, *Im Silbernen Wassergrund* (*In silvery darkness*)

Carl Rütti (b. 1949) grew up in Zug and studied the piano and organ at Zurich Conservatory and later in London. Inspired by the quality of English professional choirs, he has composed a number of large-scale *a cappella* works, several of which have been performed by the BBC Singers, the BBC Symphony Chorus, King's College Choir, and Cambridge Voices, and have been broadcast by the BBC. Rütti is also active as a pianist, organist, and teacher.

The text of this carol was written by Silja Walter, one of the most famous Swiss poets. Some of the love poems that she wrote in her 20s have become classics. In 1948 she became a nun in a closed monastery near Zurich, and she has come to be known as the most important Christian mystic writing in German. *Im Silbernen Wassergrund* is a meditation about Christmas; it invites the listener to see the events of the Nativity reflected in the ocean, which is evoked by the undulating motion of the organ part.

29. United Kingdom
Trad. arr. Bob Chilcott, *My Dancing Day*

Bob Chilcott, co-editor of this collection, has a fast-growing reputation as one of Britain's most popular and accessible composers of choral music. He has been involved in choral music for most of his life, having been a boy chorister and choral scholar in the choir of King's College, Cambridge, and also a member of the vocal group the King's Singers for 12 years. Since 1997 he has worked as a full-time composer and become involved in a growing number of workshop and conducting projects, particularly with children's and youth choirs.

This cheerful and effective *a cappella* arrangement of the traditional English carol 'Tomorrow shall be my dancing day' is published here for the first time. The piece starts simply with a soprano melody and accompanying voices, before the texture is enriched by voices in canon, voices doubled at thirds and sixths, and then voices doubled and in canon at the same time. Colourful harmonies set off the melody throughout.

30. United States of America
Rosephanye Powell, *Who is the baby?*

Since earning her undergraduate and graduate degrees in the US, Rosephanye Powell (b. 1962) has held a series of academic appointments, latterly as associate professor of voice at Auburn University in Alabama; she is also active as a soprano soloist and recitalist and a teacher. Her choral works, many of them commissioned by leading conductors in the US, have been widely published there. They include European-influenced anthems, secular choral settings, gospel songs, and arrangements of African, Caribbean, and African-American folksongs.

The first section of this carol is composed in the style of an African-American spiritual, a type of song sung in the US from the eighteenth century onwards by slaves expressing hope for freedom in this world and salvation through Jesus Christ in the spiritual world; here the music follows a call-and-response pattern. The second section is composed as a 'special' in the African-American gospel style: each voice part enters with its own rhythmic and melodic idea, which is sung simultaneously against the repeated ideas of the other voices.

31. Venezuela
Trad. arr. Alberto Grau, *Niño lindo* (*Lovely baby*)

Alberto Grau (b. 1937) was born in Spain but settled in Venezuela as a boy. As a composer, conductor, and teacher, he has earned a place among the finest Venezuelan musicians of his day. In 1967 he founded the Schola Cantorum de Caracas. He has served as a guest conductor, adjudicator, and professor of choral music in both North and South America and throughout Western Europe, and he directs choral activities in Venezuela and the Andean region.

The traditional song *Niño lindo* is a Venezuelan Christmas carol which praises the beauty of the newborn Christ child. It originated in the haciendas in the nineteenth century and uses the rhythm of the *merengue*, a dance in 2/4 metre characterized by alternating triplets and quavers. The carol would traditionally be accompanied by the *cuatro*, a small four-stringed guitar, but it appears here in a simple arrangement for four-part choir.

1. Villancico de la Falta de Fe
For a World Without Faith

Luis Rosales (1910–92)
English text: Tim Morris

EDUARDO FALÚ
(b. 1928)

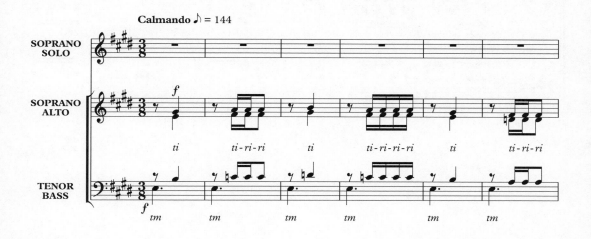

- si - ma, es _____ la es - tre - lla de Dios que guí - a
- bres tam - bién, _____ y bos - ques que a - ca - so nun - ca
__ new and bright, _____ the star of __ God that leads us
- long their way, _____ and woods that may ne - ver flow - er

ti - ri - ri ti - ri - ri - ri ti ti - ri - ri ti ti - ri - ri - ri

tm tm tm tm tm tm

ha - cia el por - tal de Be - lén.
vol - ve - rán a flo - re - cer.
to the gate of Beth - le - hem.
as the Wise Men pass them by.

ti ti - ri - ri ti ti - ri - ri - ri

(1.) Los Ma - gos, co -
(2.) Pa - san a - ños,
(1.) Be - ing wise, the
(2.) Ma - ny years and

tm tm tm tm

f

-mo son ma - gos, vie - ron la es - tre - lla na -
a - ños, a - ños, y el mun - do siem - pre los
Sa - ges saw it, as the hea - vens___ gave it
years roll on - ward, as the Wise Men___ jour - ney

-cer; los hom - bres, co - mo son hom - bres, la
ve. Con u - na lla - ga en la ma - no, ca -
but men, be - ing but men, look, but
birth; with hearts and minds___ in won - der, they

Bal - ta - sar tie - ne la
La nie - ve es mu - cha los
Bal - tha - zar has skin like
Snow is fall - ing all a -

mi - ran y no la ven.
-mi - nan-do ha - cia Be - lén.
still do not see the star.
tra - vel to Beth - le - hem.

ti - ri - ri   ti - ri - ri

Bal - ta - sar tie - ne la
La nie - ve es mu - cha los
Bal - tha - zar has skin like
Snow is fall - ing all a -

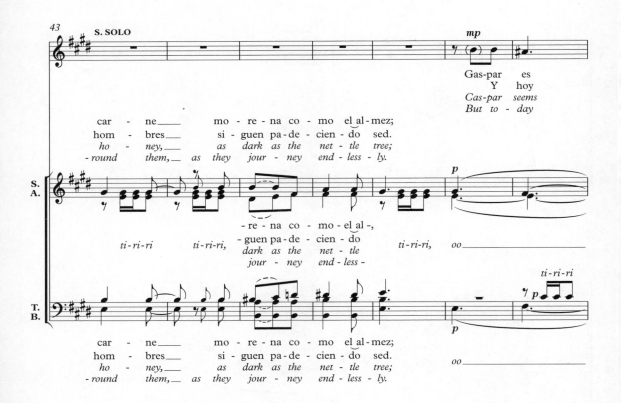

57

S. A.

-chor es   tan cre-yen-te,   tan i - lu-mi - na-do,   que   siem-pre que sus
-ve   si-gue en el   cam-po,   la san-gre si-gue en el   pie,   la es-tre - lla si -
-or   is   so   en-light-ened,   and his   faith all men in-spires   that who - e - ver
ly - ing   all   a-round them,   and their   feet   are tired and cold,   and the star still

cresc.

T. B.

cresc.

66

S. SOLO   rall.   tempo

mf

Se ven sus o - jos   ar - der.____
Pe - ro no to - dos la   ven.____
for his   eyes, they burn with   fire.____
shi-ning   out   a   light   of   gold.____

S. A.

mp   f

o - jos   mi - ran.____
-gue en el   cie - lo.____   oo_____   ti   ti-ri-ri
sees him   mar - vels,____
shines   in   hea - ven,____

T. B.

mp   f   tm   tm

75

1.   mf   2.

2. Pa-san
2. So the

ti   ti-ri-ri-ri   ti   ti-ri-ri   ti____   ti

tm   tm   tm   tm   tm____   tm____

2. Khorurd Metz
Great Mystery

English text: Bob Chilcott

Words and music by
MOVSES KHORENATSI (5th cent.)
arr. Vahram Sargsyan (b. 1981)

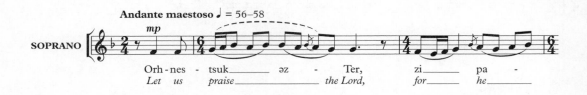

* Keyboard reduction for rehearsal only.

Breathing suggestions are editorial.

* The last bar should be sung with a closed 'n' sound.

Dedicated to The Australian Voices

3. Southern Cross

Elizabeth Anne Williams
(b. 1950)

STEPHEN LEEK
(b. 1959)

this the star the Wise Men saw, their long - est jour - ney bright - 'ning?

this the star the Wise Men saw, long - est jour - ney bright - 'ning? The

this the star the Wise Men saw, their long - est jour - ney bright - 'ning?

this the star the Wise Men saw, long - est jour - ney bright - 'ning?

Christ - mas, point - ing star still guid - ing, to

Cross shines out at Christ - mas time, its point - ing star still guid - ing.

Christ - mas, Christ - mas, point - ing star still guild - ing.

Christ - mas, Christ - mas, point - ing star still guid - ing.

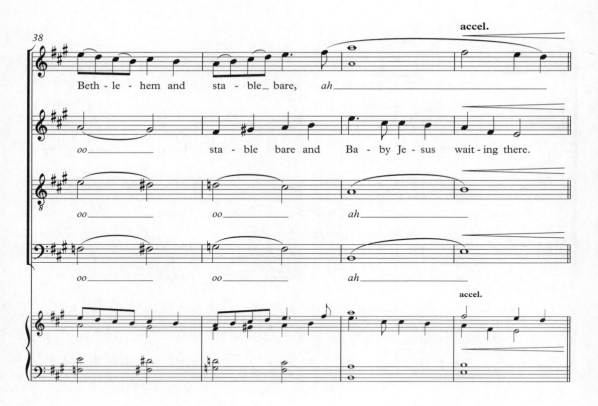

Beth - le - hem and sta - ble bare, ah

oo sta - ble bare and Ba - by Je - sus wait - ing there.

oo oo ah

oo oo ah

doo doo doo doo doo doo doo doo doo doo doo doo

doo doo doo doo doo doo doo doo doo doo doo doo doo

doo doo doo doo doo doo doo doo doo doo doo

doo doo doo doo doo doo doo doo doo doo doo doo doo doo

4. Kuttun Kantak
Night Songs

1. Gabon miresgarriak
The gentle voice of the night

Lourdes Zubeldia (b. 1923)
English text: Bob Chilcott

JAVIER BUSTO
(b. 1949)

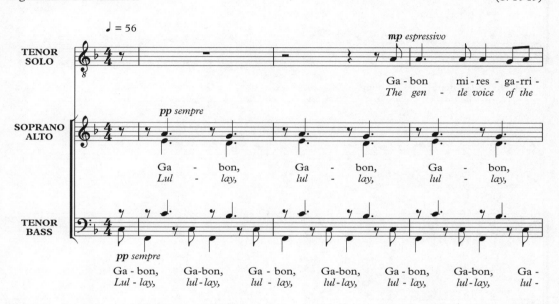

2. Gida nazu Gau ona
Give me, this Christmas night

3. Gabon izar

[English version on p. 26]

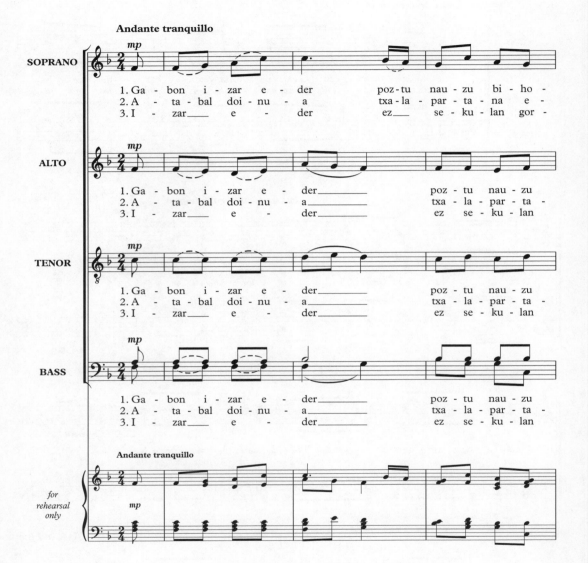

3. O lovely Christmas star

[Basque version on p. 24]

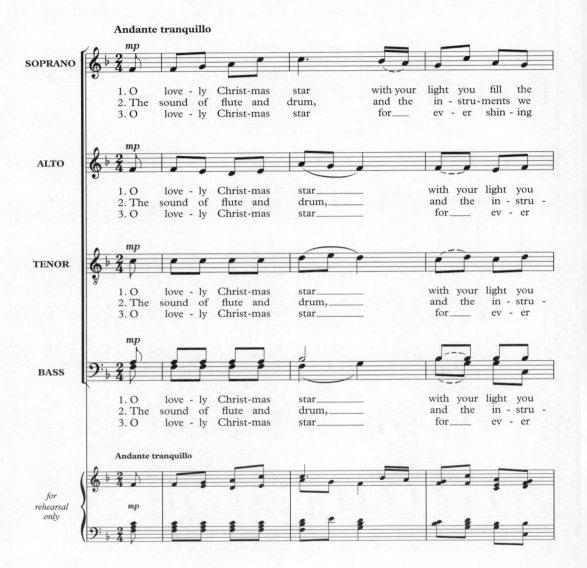

5. Nu is die roe van Jesse
The Rod of Jesse

Philippus Jennyn (d. 1670)
English text: Bob Chilcott

Flemish trad.
arr. VIC NEES (b. 1936)

1. Nu is die roe van Jes-se ge-bloeid, door Go-des zoe-ten dauw;
1. *Now has the rod of Jes-se flow'red, A gift from heav'n so rare.*

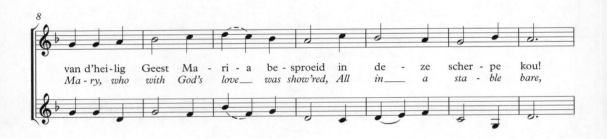

van d'hei-lig Geest Ma-ri-a be-sproeid in de-ze scher-pe kou!
Ma-ry, who with God's love was show'red, All in a sta-ble bare,

Heeft ons ge-baard haar Zoon-tje klein, een maag-den-vrucht, een Blom-me rein.
Has gi-ven us a lit-tle son, Born for us, the Ho-ly one.

2. O gro-te Heer van he-mel en aard, o Schep-per van ons al!
2. *Fa-ther of all, from hea-ven a-bove, Who came on earth be-low,*

* Cantus firmus.

* Stagger breathing.

O Jes-se blom! O zoet-ste Kind! Hoe ligt gij zo vlak in de wind.
O Je-su flow'r! O child so bright! Brought to us on this joy-ous night.

4. O Je-zu zoet, mijn op-per-ste Goed, waar-ach-tig God en mens,
4. O Je-su sweet, who came on earth, As man to pay the price,

* Keyboard reduction for rehearsal only.

6. Acalanto para o Menino Jesus
Carol for the Baby Jesus

Gerson Valle (b. 1944)
English text: Jeremy Jackman

ERNANI AGUIAR
(b. 1950)

Tranquilamente ♩ = 54

Bri - lha o céu lá de Be - lém   a es-trê - la que nos vem   e nos tráz   a men -
Bright   o'er Beth-le-hem, the   star   tells peo-ple near and   far   of the news   of sal -

-sa - gem.   Dor - me ao chão, Me - ni - no   Paz,   dei - ta-do en-tre a ni -
-va - tion.   Ox   and   ass their vi - gil   keep,   they see   a child as -

- mais, nos re - ve - la a ver - da - de.   Dor - me, traz a tu - a   paz,   di - zen-do o que nós
-leep,   and the Lord   of Cre - a - tion.   Slum - ber's peace – di-vine re - lease! – you give   to   all your

so - mos no sos - sê - go do   so - no.   Dor - me, traz a tu - a
peo - ple as your first   sa - lu - ta - tion.   Slum - ber's peace – di - vine re -

so - no traz a   Paz, Me - ni - no.
- ta-tion, may our paths be peace-ful.

7. The Huron Carol

St Jean de Brebeuf (*c*.1643)
trans. Jesse Edgar Middleton (1872–1960)

Trad., arr. ELEANOR DALEY
(b. 1955)

An arrangement of this piece for upper voices is available in *World Carols for Choirs: 29 carols for upper voices* (978–0–19–353232–8).

9 **a tempo**

Je - sus your King is born, Je - sus is born, in ex - cel - sis glo - ri - a.

8

pp ah

pp ah

S. *p* ah

A. *p* ah

T.
B. *mf unis.*

2. With - in a lodge of bro - ken bark the ten - der babe was found, a

14

rag - ged robe of rab - bit skin en - wrapped his beau - ty round; but

16 **poco rit.**

ah

ah

as the hun - ter braves drew nigh, the an - gel song rang loud and high:__

Je-sus your King is born, Je-sus is born, in ex-cel-sis glo-ri - a.

3. The ear-liest moon of win-ter-time is not so round and fair as was the ring of glo-ry on the

3. The ear-liest moon of win-ter-time is not so round and fair as was the ring of glo-ry on the

help-less in-fant there. The chiefs from far be-fore him knelt with gifts of fox and bea-ver pelt._

help-less in-fant there. The chiefs from far be-fore him knelt with gifts of fox and bea-ver pelt._

4. O

Je-sus your King is born, Je-sus is born, in ex-cel-sis glo-ri - a._

* or Tenor at pitch.

8. Notre divin Maître
Our master, Lord Jesus

Trans. Patricia Abbott   Trad., arr. GILBERT PATENAUDE
(b. 1947)

* Sopranos to sing single syllables of words sung in full by the other voices.

© Oxford University Press 2005. Photocopying this copyright material is ILLEGAL.

29

-vers. / song.

mf

Oh! Qu'il est puis - sant, au-guste, a - do - ra - ble!
Oh! He is ma - jes - tic, no - ble, and gra - cious,

-vers. / song.

mf

Oh! Qu'il est puis - sant, au-guste, a - do - ra - ble! Mais qu'il est af -
Oh! He is ma - jes - tic, no - ble, and gra-cious. Re - dee-mer most

-vers. / song.

ah

mp

au-guste, a - do - ra - ble!
Oh! no - ble, and gra - cious,

-vers. / song.

ah

mp

au-guste, a - do - ra - ble! Mais qu'il est af -
Oh! no - ble, and gra - cious. Re - dee-mer most

mf

33

mp

Hu-main, doux, ai - ma - ble, ce Dieu fait en - fant, qu'il est beau, qu'il est
come down for the right-eous; he brings us sal - va - tion, this God born for

mf   *p*

-fa - ble,
ho - ly,

oo

oo

pp   *p*

Hu-main, doux, ai - ma - ble,
come down for the right-eous;

est beau, qu'il est
this God born for

-fa - ble!
ho - ly,

pp   *p*

ce Dieu fait en - fant, qu'il est beau, qu'il est
he brings us sal - va - tion, this God born for

p

9. ¡Llega la Navidad!
Christmas is Coming

Trans. F. R. Dotseth and D. Raney

Words and melody by RAMÓN DÍAZ
(1901–76)
arr. Juan Tony Guzmán
(b. 1959)

1. El__ Ni - ño Je - sús nos tra - e__
2. Los San - tos Re - yes de O - rien - te__
1. Lit - tle Je - sus brings to us,____
2. Three kings from the O - rient seek him,

1.&2. ¡Lle-ga la Na - vi - dad!
1.&2. Joy! It is Christ-mas Day!

Percussion

The güira part may be played by small maracas, a light shaker, or egg shakers if a güira is not available. Similarly, the tambora can be replaced with a conga or tumbadora; if neither of these is available, a snare drum, with snares off, may be used.

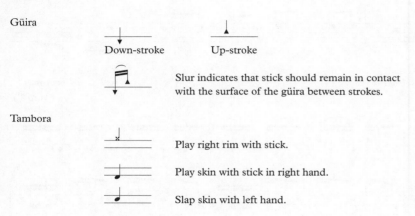

Güira

Down-stroke   Up-stroke

Slur indicates that stick should remain in contact with the surface of the güira between strokes.

Tambora

Play right rim with stick.

Play skin with stick in right hand.

Slap skin with left hand.

la__ tan de - se - a - da paz,
con__ su bue - na vo - lun - tad,
gives to us the gift of peace.
with their prai - ses and good - will;

¡Lle - ga la Na - vi - dad!
Joy! It is Christ - mas Day!

to Coda ⊕
(after final repeat)

can - té - mos-le a - gra - de - ci - dos
nos__ da - rán fe - li - ces Pas - cuas
Let__ us sing and shout ho - san - na!
bring - ing joy and ce - le - bra - tion

¡Lle-ga la Na - vi - dad!   ¡Lle-ga la Na - vi -
Joy! It is Christ-mas Day!   *Joy! It is Christ-mas*

to Coda ⊕
(after final repeat)

-lén_____ ha na - ci-do un Ni - ño_ pa - ra nues-tro bien.
-hem,_____ *born a child, the Sav - iour.* *Hon-our to his reign.*

A - la - be - mos la bon - dad_____
Let us praise_____ the good - will_____

4. A - la - be - mos la_ bon - dad_____ del Rey de los
4. Let_ us_ praise_____ the_ good - will_____ of the King of

A - la - be - mos la bon - dad
Let us praise_____ the good - will

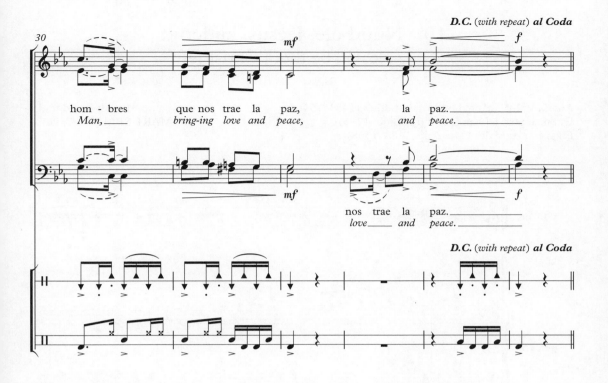

10. Nüüd ole, Jeesus, kiidetud
Now blessed be thou, Christ Jesu

Anon., V. 2–5 adapted by Martin Luther (1483–1546)
Estonian text: Johann Hornung (1660–1715)
English text: Myles Coverdale (1488–1568)

Kihnu Island trad.
arr. MART SIIMER (b. 1967)

An arrangement of this piece for upper voices is available in *World Carols for Choirs: 29 carols for upper voices* (978–0–19–353232–8).

ma - ga - mast,__ nüüd mei - e__ vae - se li - has - se on__
poor did__ lie:__ with our poor__ flesh and our poor__ blood was

tul - nud kõi - ge__ ü - lem - he - a. Küü - ri - e -
clothed that e - ver - last - ing__ good:__ Ky - rie e - lei -

- leis.
- son.

poco f

3. Nüüd i - ga - ve - ne__ päi - ke - ne pais - tab__ kõi - ge
3. E - ter - nal light doth__ now ap - pear to the world__ both

poco f

11.   Tuikkikaa, oi joulun tähtöset
Twinkle bright, you stars of Christmastide

Elsa Koponen (1885–1977)
English text: Bob Chilcott

PEKKA JUHANI HANNIKAINEN
(1854–1924)
arr. Pekka Kostiainen
(b. 1944)

1. Tuik - ki - kaa,   oi   jou - lun täh - tö - set,   kil - paa las - ten
1. *Twin - kle bright,   you   stars   of Christ - mas - tide,   twin - kle bright with*

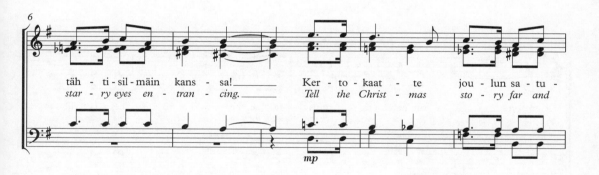

täh - ti - sil - mäin kans - sa!_____   Ker - to - kaat - te   jou - lun sa - tu -
star - ry eyes en - tran - cing._____   Tell   the Christ - mas   sto - ry far and

-a,_____   yh - tä uut - ta,   yh - tä i - ha - naa,   miel - tä viih - tä -
wide,_____   bring - ing light and   glo - ry as you shine,   in   our hearts for

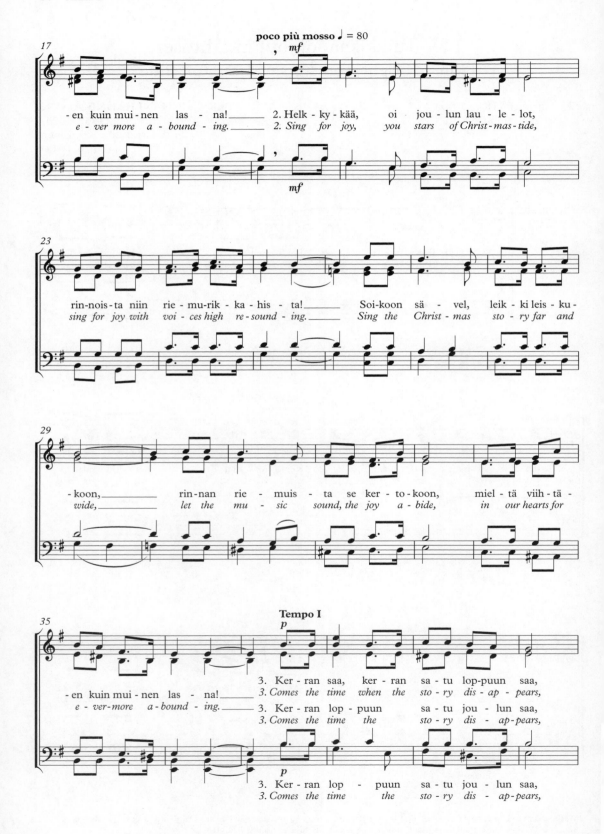

poco più mosso ♩ = 80

17

-en kuin mui-nen las-na!_____ 2. Helk-ky-kää, oi jou-lun lau-le-lot,
e-ver more a-bound-ing._____ 2. Sing for joy, you stars of Christ-mas-tide,

23

rin-nois-ta niin rie-mu-rik-ka-his-ta!_____ Soi-koon sä-vel, leik-ki leis-ku-
sing for joy with voi-ces high re-sound-ing._____ Sing the Christ-mas sto-ry far and

29

-koon,_____ rin-nan rie-muis-ta se ker-to-koon, miel-tä viih-tä-
wide,_____ let the mu-sic sound, the joy a-bide, in our hearts for

Tempo I

35

-en kuin mui-nen las-na!_____ 3. Ker-ran saa, ker-ran sa-tu lop-puun saa,
e-ver-more a-bound-ing._____ 3. Comes the time when the sto-ry dis-ap-pears,
3. Ker-ran lop-puun sa-tu jou-lun saa,
3. Comes the time the sto-ry dis-ap-pears,

3. Ker-ran lop-puun sa-tu jou-lun saa,
3. Comes the time the sto-ry dis-ap-pears,

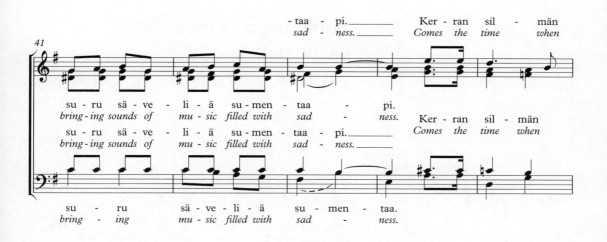

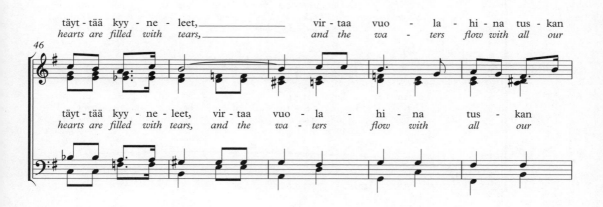

to Philip White

12. Ainsi que parmi la prée
On a hillside in the cold

Bible de Melun (1717)
English text: Jeremy Jackman

BRUNO GOUSSET
(b. 1958)

ron - de,
- pha - ne, *ah*
du - ty, ah
won - der,

2. Et que la nuit
4. Dé - plo - yant ses
2. In dark in -
4. While shep - herds

- de, fai - sait paî - tre ses a - gneaux.
- ne, fit ces - ser l'ob - scu - ri - té.
- ty, keep - ing watch o - ver their sheep.
- der, by a light as clear as day.

- de, fai - sait paî - tre ses a - gneaux. 2. Et que dé - jà la nuit
- ne, fit ces - ser l'ob - scu - ri - té. 4. Ain - si dé - plo - yant ses
- ty, keep - ing watch o - ver their sheep. 2. In the dark of night in -
- der, by a light as clear as day. 4. While the shep - herds great - ly

- bon - de, fai - sait paî - tre ses a - gneaux. 2. Et que dé - jà la nuit
- a - ne, fit ces - ser l'ob - scu - ri - té. 4. Ain - si dé - plo - yant ses
beau - ty, keep - ing watch o - ver their sheep. 2. In the dark of night in -
- sun - der, by a light as clear as day. 4. While the shep - herds great - ly

14

som - - bre   a - vait   ob - scur - ci   les   yeux,
ai - - les,   dit   le   cé - les - te   cou - rier;   *oo* _____
- tense, _____   *all   was   hid - den   from   the   eye:*   *oo* _____
fear'd, _____   *God's   all - glo - rious   heav'n - ly   throng,*

mf

2. Et d'une   é - pais - se   fu -
4. Et puis   re - prit   sa   vo -
2. Not   the   faint - est   light   at
4. And   an   ang - el   did   de -

sombre   de   son   ombre   a - vait   ob - scur - ci   les   yeux,
ailes   im - mor - telles,   dit   le   cé - les - te   cou - rier;   *oo* _____
- tense,   blind - ing   sense,   all   was   hid - den   from   the   eye: *oo* _____
fear'd,   there   ap - pear'd,   God's   all - glor - ious   heav'n - ly   throng,

som - - bre,
ai - - les,   *oo* _____
- tense, _____   *oo* _____
fear'd, _____

5. ah_____
8. ah_____

5. ah_____
8. ah_____

5. ah_____
8. ah_____

(5.) - vous, troupe en - dor - mie,   de Sy - rie,   le - vez - vous tous à la
(8.) pas - teurs, à cette heure,   sans de - meure,   en Beth - lé - em la ci -
(5.) *more a - bout your   beds,   slee - py - heads,   shep - herds   stir your - selves I*
(8.) *shep - herds haste a - way,   no de - lay,   and in   Beth - le - hem you'll*

ah_____ ah_____
ah_____ ah_____

ah_____ ah_____
ah_____ ah_____ the
ah_____ ah_____ re -

ah_____
ah_____
ah_____ ah_____ the
ah_____ re -

fois, rom-pez, rom-pez la pa - resse, qui vous presse, et ve - nez ou - ïr ma
-té; al - lez, bri - ga - de cham - pêtre, re - con - naître l'heure de sa na - ti - vi -
pray, cast all sloth - ful - ness a - way, no dis - may, hear the news I bring to -
find, ly - ing in a man - ger bare, sleep - ing there, the re - deem - er of man -

6. Voi - ci l'heu-reu - se nui - tée, dé - si - rée de tou-
9. D'u - ne lé - gè - re se - cousse, à la course, l'un va
6. For this is the night of grace, in this place, which the
9. Let each one of you take heart, play your part, make your

(ah) _____
(ah) _____

____ à ma voix. 6. Voi - ci l'heu-reu - se nui - tée, dé - si - rée de tou-
sa na - ti - vi - té. 9. D'u - ne lé - gè - re se - cousse, à la course, l'un va
news I bring to - day. 6. For this is the night of grace, in this place, which the
- deem - er of man - kind. 9. Let each one of you take heart, play your part, make your

____ à ma voix. 6. Voi - ci l'heu-reu - se nui - tée, dé - si - rée de tou-
sa na - ti - vi - té. 9. D'u - ne lé - gè - re se - cousse, à la course, l'un va
news I bring to - day. 6. For this is the night of grace, in this place, which the
- deem - er of man - kind. 9. Let each one of you take heart, play your part, make your

quasi port.

voix.
- té.   6. *ah* _____
- day.   9. *ah* _____
- kind.

p

* Small notes apply to verse 8 only.

38

-te l'an-ti-qui-té,   où le cé-les-te Mes-sie,   re-çoit vi-e,
l'autre ai-guil-lon-nant, et tous sous mê-me con-duite, d'u-ne sui-te, *ah*____
*pro-phets long fore-saw,   and the hour so long a-wait-ed, now do-nat-ed, ah*____
way with sim-ple joy: on-ward shep-herds, now de-part, light of heart,

-te l'an-ti-qui-té,   où le cé-les-te Mes-sie,   re-çoit vi-e, con-jointe
l'autre ai-guil-lon-nant, et tous sous mê-me con-duite, d'u-ne sui-te, trou-vent
pro-phets long fore-saw,   and the hour so long a-wait-ed, now do-nat-ed, is to
way with sim-ple joy: on-ward shep-herds, now de-part, light of heart, to sa-

-te l'an-ti-qui-té,   où le cé-les-te Mes-si - e,   *ah*____
l'autre ai-guil-lon-nant, et tous sous mê-me con-dui - te, *ah*____
*pro-phets long fore-saw,   and the hour so long a-wait - ed, ah*____
*way with sim-ple joy: on-ward shep-herds, now de-part,*____

*(ah)*____   où le Mes-sie,____ re-çoit vi-e, con-jointe
*(ah)*____   *et sous mê-me con-dui - te,____ trou-vent*
*(ah)*____   *and the hour a-wait - ed, is to*
        on-ward shep-herds, now   de-part, to sa-

58

-gnie s'hu - mi - lie et se cour-be de -vant lui; cha-cun d'eux hum-ble l'a -
town, kneel-ing down, then their hearts be- gan to sing, and with a - dor - a - tion

-gnie s'hu - mi - lie et se cour-be de -vant lui; cha-cun d'eux hum-ble l'a -
town, kneel-ing down, then their hearts be- gan to sing, and with a - dor - a - tion

p
(ah) _____ et se cour-be de-vant lui; _____ cha - cun
then their hearts be- gan to sing, and with

mp
(ah) _____ cha - cun d'eux hum-ble l'a -
and with a - dor - a - tion

63

pp
-dore, et l'ho - nore, et le ca-resse à l'en -vi. _____ 12. Cha - cun _____
fir'd, love-in- spir'd, they re - ver'd the in-fant King. _____ 12. Each brought _____

pp
-dore, et l'ho - nore, et le ca-resse à l'en - vi, a l'en - vi. 12. oo _____
fir'd, love-in- spir'd, they re - ver'd the in-fant King, in-fant King.

mp
d'eux l'ho - nore à l'en - vi. _____ 12. Cha-cun de main pas-to -
love they re - ver'd the in - fant King. _____ 12. Each had brought some lit - tle

p
-dore, et l'ho - nore, et le ca-resse à l'en - vi, à l'en - vi. 12. Cha-cun de main pas-to -
fir'd, love-in- spir'd, they re - ver'd the in-fant King, in-fant King. 12. Each had brought some lit - tle

13. Süßer die Glocken nie klingen

[English version on p. 84]

Trad., arr. KARSTEN GUNDERMANN
(b. 1966)

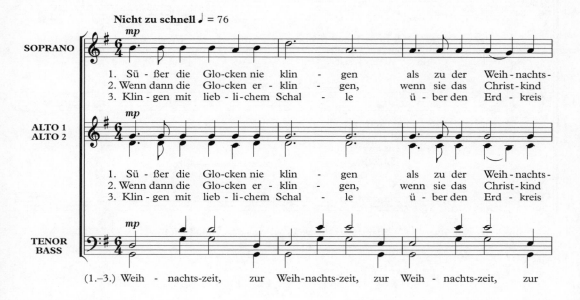

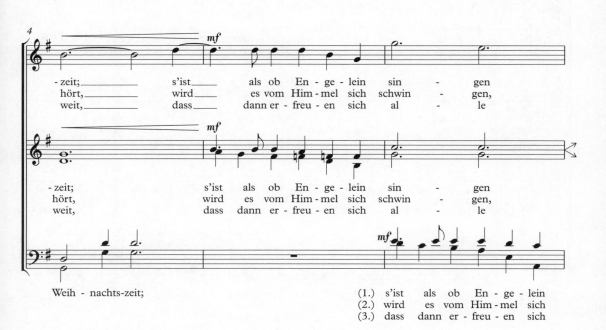

13. Sweetly the Bells are Ringing

[German version on p. 81]

Trad.
English text: Bob Chilcott

Trad., arr. KARSTEN GUNDERMANN
(b. 1966)

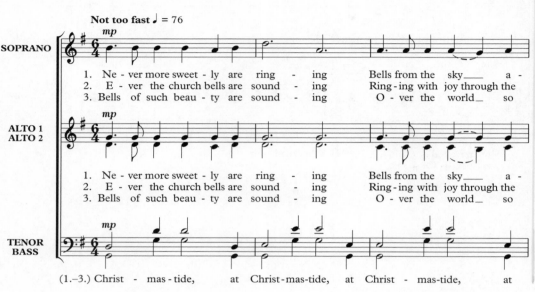

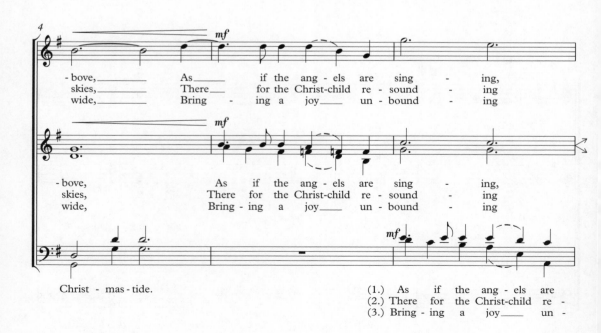

14. Krismas dodzi vo
Christmas Time is Here

Trans. David Blackwell

Words and music by
ROBERT M. KWAMI
(1954–2004)

Slower ♩. = 72

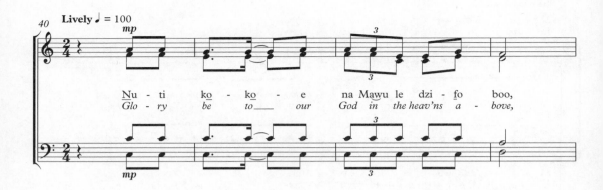

15. Nagykarácsony Éjszakáján
On Great Christmas Night

English text: Tim Morris

Trad., arr. MIKLÓS KOCSÁR
(b. 1933)

zöld ág,   ki - rá - lyi___ nem - ből___ nagy mél - tó - ság.___
- szol - ban,   bé - ta - kar - gat - va___ posz - tócs - ká - ban.___
rose stem,   from the an - cient house of___ Beth - le - hem.___
man - ger,   shel - tered from the cold___ and___ dan - ger.___

zöld ág,   ki - rá - lyi___ nem - ből mél - tó - ság.___
- szol - ban,   bé - ta - kar - gat - va posz - tócs - ká - ban.___
rose stem,   from the an - cient house of Beth - le - hem.___
man - ger,   shel - tered from the cold___ and dan - ger.___

ág,   ki - rá - lyi___ nagy mél - tó - nagy mél - tó - ság.
- ban,   bé - ta - kar - va posz - tócs - ká - posz - tócs - ká - ban.
stem,   from the an - cient house of, of Beth - le - hem.
- ly,   *shel - tered from___ the cold___ and dan - ger.*

ág,   ki - rá - lyi___ nagy mél - tó - ság.___
- ban,   bé - ta - kar - va posz - tócs - ká - ban.___
stem,   from the house of Beth - le - hem.___
- ly,   *shel - tered from___ the dan - ger.___*

3. Ö - kör, sza - már rá - ja le - he - lé - nek, mert tag - ja - i hi - deg -
3. See his bo - dy shak - ing with___ the cold; with their warmth the ox and

28

-től resz-ket - nek.   Ma - dár - kák, kik   fö - löt - te rep - des - nek,
ass__ en - fold,   while a - bove him,   in__ their__ joy,__

-től resz-ket nek.__   Ma - dár - kák, kik__ rep - des - nek,
ass__ en - fold,__   while a - bove him,__ ce - le - brate

poco rit.   **p**

34

és__ mind - nyá - jan__ ör - ven - dez - nek.
flutt' - ring birds__ sing to the ba - by boy.__

és__ mind-nyá - jan ör - vend -, ör - ven - dez - nek.
flutt' - ring birds__ sing, ba - by, the ba - by boy.

mp

és__ mind-nyá - jan ör - vend - nek.__
flutt' - ring birds__ sing, ba - by boy.__

p

Andante ♩ = 80

39   **p (mf)**   *cresc. poco a poco al* **f**

4. Menny - ből az an - gyal le - jött hoz - zá - tok,
5. Is - ten - nek fi - a, ki ma szü - le - tett
4. *See now the ang - el comes to the shep - herds*
5. *God's son is ly - ing there in a low - ly*

p (mf)   *cresc. poco a poco al* **f**

43

pász - to - rok,   pász - to - rok,
já - szol - ban,   já - szol - ban,
out of heav'n,   out of heav'n,
ox - en stall,   ox - en stall,

hogy Bet - le - hem - be   si - et - ve   men - vén
ő   le - szen nék - tek   üd - vö - zí - tő - tök
quick - ly they foll - ow,   as   they were told,   to
but he has come to   earth to re - deem   and

hogy Bet - le - hem - be   si - et - vén
ő   le - szen nék - tek,   ő   le - szen
quick - ly they foll - ow,   they go to
but he has come here,   has come to

hogy Bet - le - hem - be   si - et - ve   men - vén
ő   le - szen nék - tek   üd - vö - zí - tő - tök
quick - ly they foll - ow,   as   they were told,   to
but he has come to   earth to re - deem   and

hogy Bet - le - hem - be   si - et - vén
ő   le - szen nék - tek,   ő   le - szen
quick - ly they foll - ow,   they go to
but he has come here,   has come to

lás - sá - tok,   lás - sá - tok.
va - ló - ban,   va - ló - ban.
Beth - le - hem,   Beth - le - hem.
save you all,   save you all.

Con moto ♩ = 104

6. Kis - ka - rá - csony, nagy-ka - rá - csony, ki - sült - e már   a ka - lá - csom?
7. Nagy-ka - rá - csony   éj - sza - ká - ján, jé - zus szü - le - té - se nap - ján,
6. *Lit - tle Je - sus,*   *great_ Je - sus,*   *our_ hearts*   *wor-ship him,_*
7. *On the night of*   *great_ Christ - mas,* *on his birth - day,* *on this day,_*

ha ki - sült már,   i - de vé - le,   hadd e - gyem meg   me - le - gé - be.
ör - ven - dez - zünk,   vi - ga - doz - zunk,   meg-szü - le - tett   kis Jé - zu - sunk.
lit - tle Je - sus,   *great_ Je - sus,*   *our_ Lord and*   *our_ King._*
let us sing and   *ce - le - brate him,* *lit - tle Je - sus*   *born to - day._*

poco rit.   **poco meno**

Ör - ven - dez - zünk,   vi - ga - doz - zunk,   meg - szü - le - tett
Let us sing and   *ce - le - brate him,*   *lit - tle Je - sus,*

allargando

kis Jé - zu - sunk._   *ah_*   *ah.*
lit - tle Je - sus._

kis Jé - zu - sunk._
lit - tle Je - sus._   *ah._*

16.   Immanúel oss í nátt
Emmanuel, to us this night

Gudmundur Högnason
from *Hymnodia Sacra*, 1742
English text: Bob Chilcott

ÞORKELL SIGURBJÖRNSSON
(b. 1938)

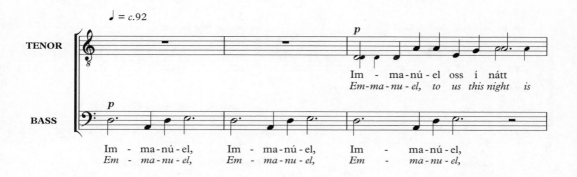

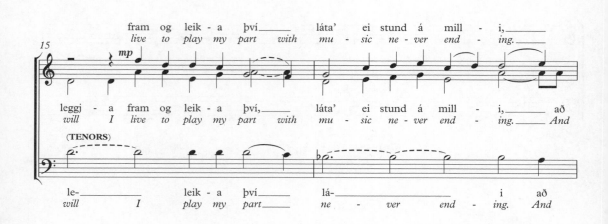

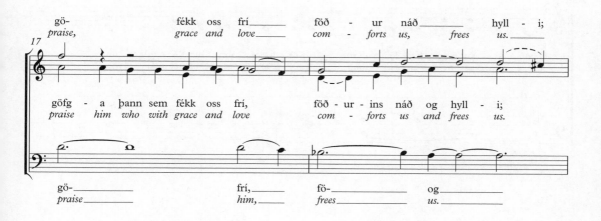

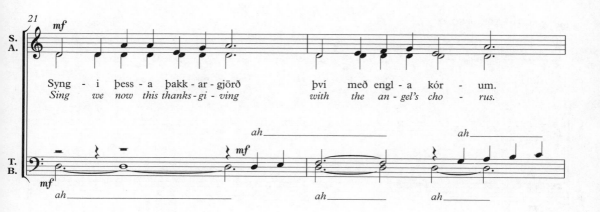

23

Heið - ur, lof og há - leit dýrð____ sé hæst - um Guð - i vór - um.
Ho - nour, praise from man li - ving____ to the God be - fore us.

(*ah*)_____

*ah*____ *ah*____

25

Feng - inn er nú fyrst á jörð___ frið - ur smám og stór - um.___
Now for all man - kind on earth__ peace a - new is gi - ven.__

27

Fað - ir - inn elsk - ar aum - a hjörð,___ oss sem villt - ir fór - um.___
By__ the Sa - viour's won - drous birth__ we are all for - gi - ven.__

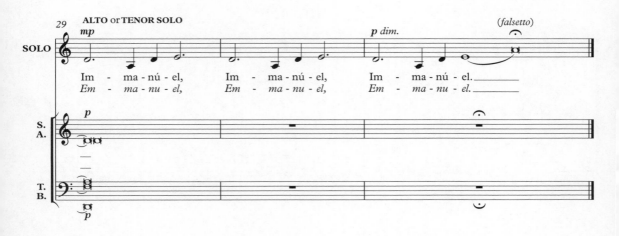

29 **ALTO** or **TENOR SOLO**

mp   *p dim.*   (*falsetto*)

SOLO

Im - ma - nú - el, Im - ma - nú - el, Im - ma - nú - el.___
Em - ma - nu - el, Em - ma - nu - el, Em - ma - nu - el.___

S.
A.

p

T.
B.

p

17. Carúl Fáilte
A Carol of Welcome

Words and music by
SÉAMAS DE BARRA
(b. 1955)

1. Fáil - te romhat a___ Rí na bhflaith - eas, Fáil - te romhat a___
1. Wel - come be thou___ King___ of heav - en, Wel - come be thou___

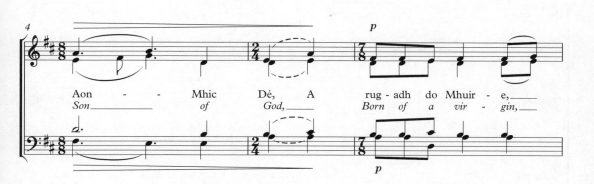

Aon - - Mhic Dé, A rug - adh do Mhuir - e,___
Son___ of God,___ Born of a vir - gin,

má - thair 'gus maigh - dean, Chun go sá - bhál - fá___ sinn___ ón
Ma - ry our moth - er, For to pre - serve___ us___ all___ from

olc,_____ ón olc,_____ ón olc,_____ ón olc._____

ill,_____ from ill,_____ from ill,_____ from ill._____

S.
Fáil - te, fáil - - - te, fáil - te romhat a Aon-Mhic Dé, fáil -
Wel-come, wel - - - come, wel-come be thou Son of God, wel -

A.
Fáil - te, fáil - - - te, fáil - te romhat a Aon-Mhic Dé, fáil -
Wel-come, wel - - - come, wel-come be thou Son of God, wel -

T.
Fáil - te romhat a_____ Rí na bhflaith-eas, fáil - te romhat a Aon-Mhic Dé, fáil -
Wel-come be thou_ King of heav - en, wel-come be thou Son of God, wel -

B.
Fáil - te romhat a_____ Rí na bhflaith-eas, fáil - te romhat a Aon-Mhic Dé, fáil -
Wel-come be thou_ King of heav - en, wel-come be thou Son of God, wel -

* Keyboard reduction for rehearsal only.

Christ-us na - tus est, Ho - di - e, Ho - di - e, Ho - di - e,

Ho - di - e Christ-us na - - tus est,

Ho - di - e, Ho - di - e! Ho - di - e! 2. Fáil - te romhat a 2. Wel - come be thou

Ho - di - e, Ho - di - e!

Rí na n-aing-eal A thán - aig go teach na bpian a - nuas, 'S a
King of an - gels Who came from a - bove to the place of pain, And

chod-ail i stáb - la___ bocht go humh - al, Chun go sá - bhál - fá___
hum - bly slept in a sta - ble low - ly, For to pre - serve___ us___

sinn___ ón olc, ón olc, ón olc,___ ón olc.
all___ from ill,___ from ill,___ from ill,___ from ill.___

S.

Fáil - te, fáil - - - te, fáil - te romhat a Aon-Mhic Dé, fáil -
Wel - come, wel - - - come, wel - come be thou Son of God, wel -

A.

Fáil - te, fáil - - - te, fáil - te romhat a Aon-Mhic Dé, fáil -
Wel - come, wel - - - come, wel - come be thou Son of God, wel -

T.

Fáil - te romhat a___ Rí na naing-eal, fáil - te romhat a Aon-Mhic Dé, fáil -
Wel - come be thou___ King of an - gels, wel - come be thou Son of God, wel -

B.

Fáil - te romhat a___ Rí na naing-eal, fáil - te romhat a Aon-Mhic Dé, fáil -
Wel - come be thou___ King of an - gels, wel - come be thou Son of God, wel -

18. Infant Joy

William Blake (1757–1827)

RIKUYA TERASHIMA
(b. 1964)

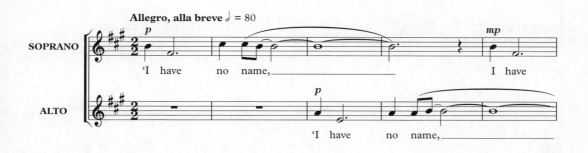

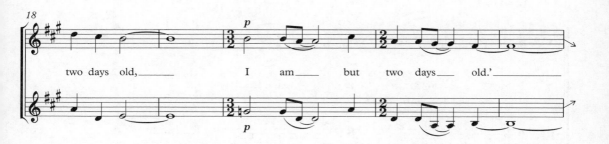

19. Jajang, jajang, Ahgi Yesu
Lullay, lullay, Baby Jesu

English text: Bob Chilcott

Words and music by
HYUN CHUL LEE
(b. 1973)

Nat - go,_____ Nat-go na - zun i ddang-eu - ro.____
He_ came,_____ He came down_ to show us his love.____

Nat - go,_____ Nat-go na - zun i ddang-eu - ro.____
He_ came,_____ He came down_ to show us his love.____

Nat - go,____ Nat-go na - zun i ddang-eu - ro.____
He_ came,____ He came down_ to show us his love.____

Nat - go, Nat-go na - zun i ddang-eu - ro.____
He came, He came down_ to show us his love.____

rit.   **Tempo I**

Nae - ryu oh - syun - ne._____
Here on earth to save us.____

Ja - jang,   ja - jang,____
Lul - lay,   lul - lay,____

Ja - jang, ja - jang, ja - jang, ja - jang,
Lul - lay, lul - lay, lul - lay, lul - lay,

rit.   **Tempo I**

20.   Dedziet skalu, pūtiet guni
Bring us fire, bring us light

English text: Bob Chilcott

Trad. arr. SELGA MENCE (b. 1953)

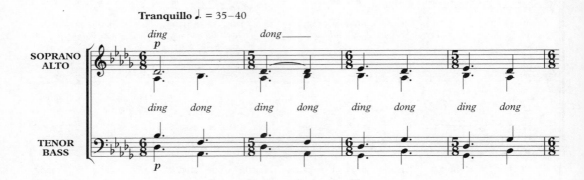

De-dziet ska - lu,___ pū - tiet___ gu - ni,   Lai - diet   die - vu   is - ta - bā!
Bring us   fire,___   bring us___   light,_   Let___   God in - to   your heart!

* Keyboard reduction for rehearsal only.

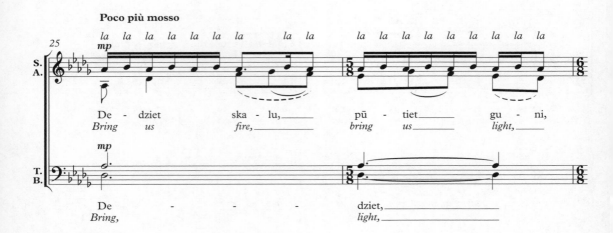

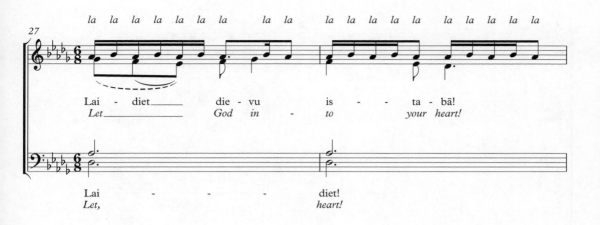

De-dziet ska - lu,___ pū - tiet___ gu - ni, Lai - diet___ die - vu is - ta - bā!
Bring us fire,___ bring us___ light, _ Let___ God in - to your heart!

21. Lullaby Carol

15th-cent. English

DAVID HAMILTON
(b. 1955)

22. Amuworo ayi otu nwa
For unto us a child is born

Isaiah 9: 6

CHRISTIAN ONYEJI
(b. 1967)

An arrangement of this piece for upper voices is available in *World Carols for Choirs: 29 carols for upper voices* (978–0–19–353232–8).

nye-wo-r'a-yi.＿   O - tu＿ nwa＿ ka e nye-wo-r'a - yi,＿
us a Son's giv'n.＿   Un - to＿ us,＿ un - to a child's born,

ka e nye-wo - r'a - yi.
un - to us a Son's giv'n.

o - tu＿ nwa＿ ka e nye-wo-r'a - yi.＿   O - tu＿ nwa nwo-ke ka e
un - to＿ us,＿ un - to us a child's born.＿   Un - to us a Son, un - to

nye-wo - r'a - yi,＿   o - tu＿ nwa＿ ka e nye-wo-r'a - yi.＿
us a Son's giv'n,＿   un - to＿ us,＿ un - to us a Son's giv'n.

N'i - hi n'a -
For un-to

n'i - hi n'a mu-wo-r'a-yi o-tu＿ nwa.   O - tu＿ nwa nwo-ke, ka e
for＿ un-to us now a child is＿ born.   Un - to＿ us a Son, un - to

- mu-wo-r'a-yi o-tu＿ nwa,
us now a child is＿ born,

23.   Det hev ei rose sprunge
A spotless rose

Anon. German (1587)
Norwegian text: P. Hognestad (1921)
English text: C. Winkworth (1869)

OLA GJEILO
(b. 1978)

* Or group of sopranos.

An arrangement of this piece for upper voices is available in *World Carols for Choirs: 29 carols for upper voices* (978–0–19–353232–8).

24. Hej, hej, lelija!

[English version on p. 155]

Polish trad.
arr. STANISŁAW SZCZYCIŃSKI (b. 1954)

24. Hey, hey, lily

[Polish version on p. 154]

Trad.
English text: Bob Chilcott

Polish trad.
arr. STANISŁAW SZCZYCIŃSKI (b. 1954)

25. Ena noč polna veselja
On a starlit night

English text: Tim Morris

Trad., arr. MAKSIMILJAN FEGUŠ
(b. 1948)

to next page for vv. 2–5

Ena noč polna veselja
On a starlit night

2. Kar je Eva nam zgubila skoz svojo pregrešnostjo,
    je Marija zadobila skoz svojo ponižnostjo.
    *Ena mati je postala
    ven dar dvica je ostala.

Refrain
    Veselimo se vsi skupaj tega rojstva Božjega.
    Veselimo se vsi skupaj tega rojstva Božjega.

3. V eni štalci je bil rojen kralj nebes ino zemle
    v ene jasli je položen, kir gospod je čez use.
    Oj ponižnost, božja milost,
    nas lepo uči ponižnost.

[Refrain]

4. Kir pastirci tam na polji so živinco vahtali,
    so njih angelci budili, de je bilo polnoči.
    'Hitro pojte no poglejte,'
    'kaj je v štalci za no dejte!'

[Refrain]

5. Čast bodi Bogu Očetu ino Duhu Svetemu,
    čast bod Božjemu Sinu na ta svet rojenemu
    ino čast tebi, Marija
    k si rodila Jezusa!

[Refrain]

2. When she gave the fruit to Adam, Eve was cursed for her sin,
    but the lowliness of Mary opened heav'n's gate, let us in.
    *Still a virgin, though a mother,
    so we sing one to another:

Refrain
    Come, rejoice and sing together, celebrate his holy birth.
    Come, rejoice and sing together, celebrate his holy birth.

3. For the grace of God so gentle teaches us humility,
    and the king of heav'n eternal sits on Mary's humble knee.
    With the oxen in a stable,
    he was born—see, 'tis no fable:

[Refrain]

4. To the shepherds in the meadows, as they kept their flocks
        by night,
    came an angel bearing tidings, who, encircled by great light,
    bade them hasten to the stable,
    run as fast as they were able:

[Refrain]

5. Glory be to God the Father, glory be to God the Son,
    glory to the Holy Spirit, Lord eternal, Three in One.
    Glory to his blessed Mother,
    for like her there is no other:

[Refrain]

* The third line of each verse is sung by the tenors and basses (bars 8–10), and the fourth line by the sopranos and altos (bars 10–12).

Commissioned by the Creative Arts Foundation.
For my father

26. Susa ninna

Words and music by
PETER LOUIS VAN DIJK
(b. 1953)

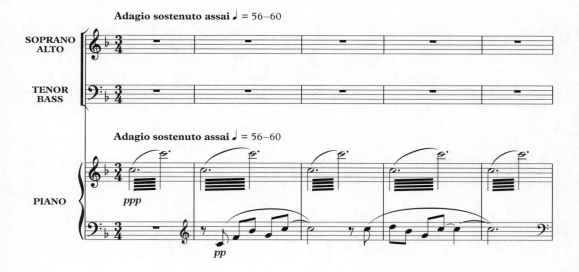

Aand - ster,___ lei ons met jou hel-der
Lead us,___ eve - ning star, with your clear

There are two additional accompaniments for this carol: 1) for orchestra and 2) for organ and brass ensemble. Scores and parts for both versions are available to hire from the publisher.

An arrangement of this piece for upper voices is available in *World Carols for Choirs: 29 carols for upper voices* (978–0–19–353232–8).

noe, su - sa, kind - jie, maak jou, nin - na___ o - gies
noo, *su - sa,* *ba - by,* *close your nin - na___ eyes now,*

toe.___
do.___

Aand - ster,___ lei ons deur dié don-ker
Lead us,___ eve - ning star, through this dark

37

cresc. poco a poco   T.   *f*   *dim. poco a poco*

nag   weer na   Gol - go - tha, waar Je - sus steeds wag: die   kruis waar   Hy   seë - vier oor die
night   back to   Gol - go - tha, where Je - sus still waits: the   cross where   he   tri - umphs o - ver

B.

42 *unis.*   T.   *molto*

dood se bit – ter mag en   waar eng - e - le   sing:
death's bit – ter might and   where ang - els still   sing:

B.

sfp   sfp   sfp   *molto*

46 **ff** *unis.*   3   3   3

S.
A.

Al - le - lu - ia!_____ Al - le - lu - ia!_____   Dit is___ vol-bring! Al -
Al - le - lu - ia!_____ Al - le - lu - ia!_____   Now all is ful-filled! Al -

T.
B.

ff *unis.*   3   3   3

ff   3   3   3

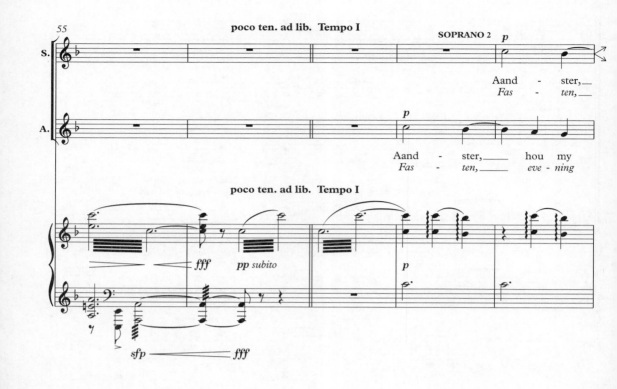

su-sa, kind-jie,   maak jou, nin-na_____ o - gies toe.____
su-sa, ba - by,   *close your nin-na_____ eyes now, do.____*

noe,
noo,

27. Ett Nyfött Barn
A Newborn Child

Christer Åsberg (b. 1940)
English text: Bob Chilcott

ROBERT SUND
(b. 1942)

An orchestration of the accompaniment for woodwind (2.2.2.2), glockenspiel, and strings is available to hire from the publisher.

An arrangement of this piece for upper voices is available in *World Carols for Choirs: 29 carols for upper voices* (978–0–19–353232–8).

stal - lets skjul._____ Och stjär - nan ser långt bor - ti -
jor - den bär._____ En natt tar slut, en dag har
laid____ in hay._____ The star is watch - ing from a -
Pa - ra - dise._____ The night de - parts, a new day

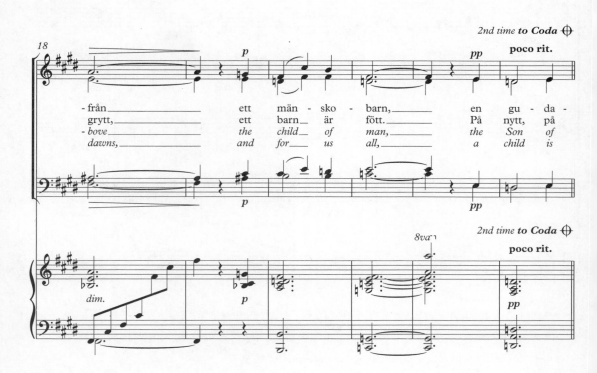

- från_____ ett män - sko - barn,_____ en gu - da -
grytt,_____ ett barn___ är fött._____ På nytt, på
- bove_____ the child___ of man,_____ the Son of
dawns,_____ and for___ us all,_____ a child is

2nd time **to Coda** ⊕
poco rit.

28. Im Silbernen Wassergrund
In silvery darkness

Silja Walter (b. 1919)
English text: Jeremy Jackman

CARL RÜTTI
(b. 1949)

An orchestration of the accompaniment for harp and strings is available to hire from the publisher.

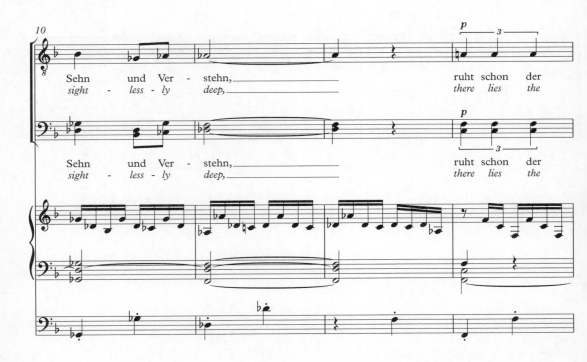

Him - mel in dir, Mensch. Spielt er sein Heil - spiel mit
still - ness of hea - ven. There is the joy of sal -

Him - mel in dir, Mensch. Spielt er sein Heil - spiel mit
still - ness of hea - ven. There is the joy of sal -

dir, Mensch, schließt er die Hoch - zeit mit dir, Mensch.
- va - tion. There is the key to your wed - lock,

dir, Mensch, schließt er die Hoch - zeit mit dir, Mensch.
- va - tion. There is the key to your wed - lock,

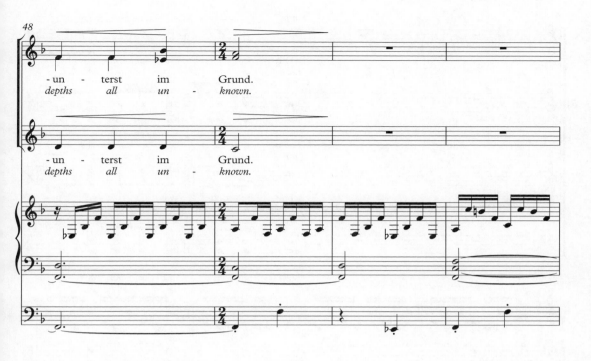

- un - terst im Grund.
depths all un - known.

- un - terst im Grund.
depths all un - known.

for the North Cotswold Chamber Choir

29. My Dancing Day

English trad.
arr. BOB CHILCOTT (b. 1955)

30. Who is the baby?

Words and music by
ROSEPHANYE POWELL
(b. 1962)

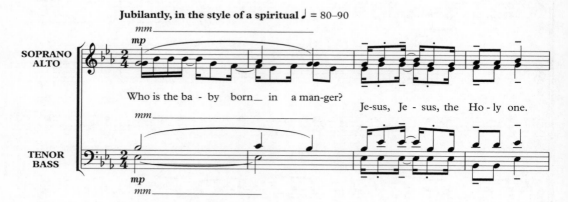

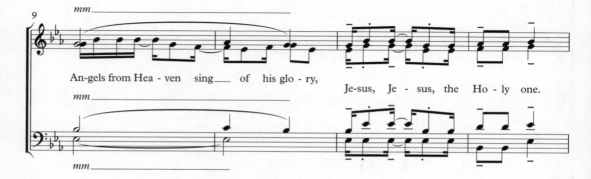

Verses may be sung by a soloist or small group.

An arrangement of this piece for upper voices is available in *World Carols for Choirs: 29 carols for upper voices* (978–0–19–353232–8).

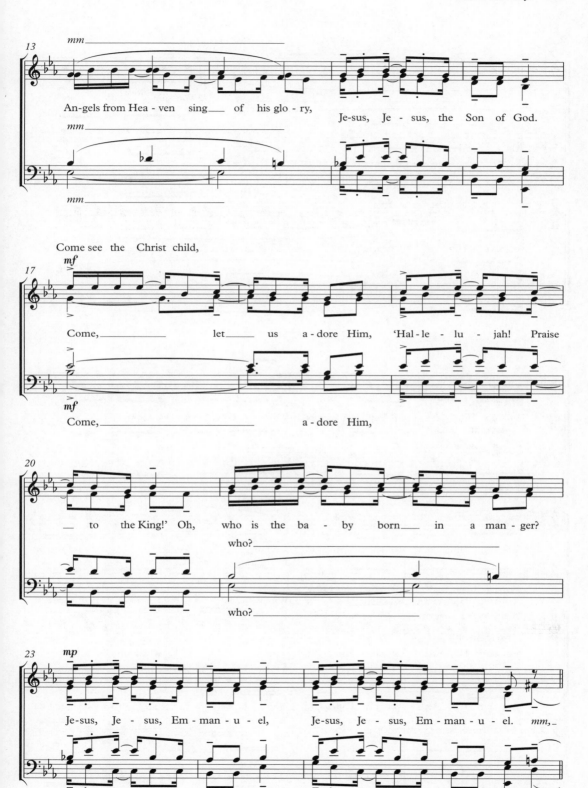

* Optional clap on beat two. Continue clapping through to the end.

† Keyboard reduction for rehearsal only.

Gospel style ♩ = ♪♪

55

B. Come,_____ let_ us sing praise, sing praise_ to the ba - by. Come, let's praise the

60

T. Oh, come let us sing! Oh, come let us

B. ba - by born in Beth - le - hem._ Oh, come,_____ let_ us sing

65

praise! Oh, come let us sing and praise the Ho - ly one. born in Beth-le-hem.

praise, sing praise to the ba - by. Come, let's praise the ba - by born in Beth-le - hem.

70

A. Hal-le - lu-jah! Hal-le - lu-jah! Hal-le - lu-jah!

T. Oh, come let us sing! Oh, come let us praise!

B. _ Oh, come,_____ let_ us sing praise, sing praise

(optional repeat)

31. Niño lindo
Lovely baby

English text: Tim Morris

Venezuelan trad.
arr. ALBERTO GRAU (b. 1937)

1. E - sa tu her-mo - su - ra, e - se tu can - dor el al - ma me
2. Con tus o - jos lin - dos, Je-sús, mi - ra - me y so - lo con
3. Ad - iós, tier-no In - fan - te, ad-iós, ni-ño ad - iós, ad-iós, dul-ce a -

ro - ba, el al - ma me ro - ba, me ro-ba el a - mor.
e - so, y so - lo con e - so, me con - so - la - ré.
-man - te, ad-iós, dul-ce a - man - te, ad-iós, ni-ño ad - iós.

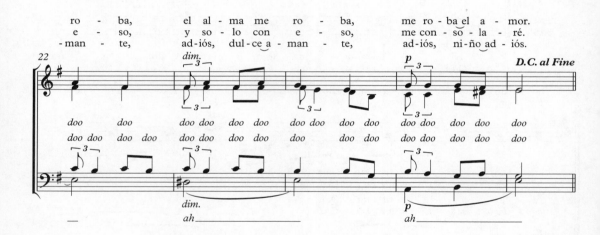

English verses:

1. For it is your fairness,
   and your innocence,
   and your soul that captures,
   and your soul that captures,
   captures my heart.

2. Look upon me, Jesus,
   with your gentle eyes;
   only looking at me,
   only looking at me,
   will you comfort me.

3. So farewell, sweet infant,
   so farewell, my child;
   so farewell, my dear one,
   so farewell, my dear one,
   so farewell, my child.

APPENDIX
Pronunciation guides

These pronunciation guides have been designed as a tool for English-language choirs who wish to sing non-English carol texts. As such, the guides are not exhaustive, but rather provide basic explanations of the sounds needed to sing each text. Particularly for more unfamiliar languages, choirs may wish to use the guides in conjunction with advice from native speakers.

Arranged alphabetically according to language, the guides are broken down into individual sounds—typically vowels, consonants, and combinations of vowels and consonants—and/or approximations of whole words, according to the approach that best suits each language; in some cases, example words have been given from the carol texts. Sounds are compared to English words (e.g., 'o' as in 'cot'), except where no English equivalent exists, when well-known words have been selected from other languages (e.g., 'u' as in German 'über'). Where no explanation is given, it may be assumed that a sound is pronounced as in English.

Afrikaans (South Africa)

Vowels

a	as in 'apple' (short)
aa	as 'a' in 'are' (long)
e	as in 'met' except in *terug*, *gerig*, and *geprys*, where it sounds like 'uh'; in *herder*, where it sounds like 'air'; and in *Jesus*, where it sounds as 'ee' in 'seed'
ee	as 'ei' in 'weir'
eë	as in 'seer'
ei	as 'ay' in 'hay'
eu	as 'e' in 'dear'
i	as in 'bitter' except in *gerig* and the second 'i' in *veilig*, where it sounds like 'uh'
ie	as in German 'die'
ié	as 'ie' above, but with greater stress
o	as 'a' in 'awning' in *volbring* and *ons*; as 'oo' in 'boor' in *ogies* and *Koning*
oe	as 'oo' in 'hoop'
oë	like 'ooh-wuh'
oo	as in 'boor'
ou	like 'oh'
u	as 'i' in 'bitter' except in *terug*, where it sounds as in 'bug', and in *susa*, where it sounds as in German 'über'
ui	as 'a' in 'brace', thus *kruis* is pronounced 'krace'

Consonants

d	as in 'dog' except in *kindjie*, where it is silent, and in *Heiland*, where it becomes a soft 't'
g	guttural, like the 'ch' in 'loch'
h	as in 'hot' except in *Bethlehem*, where it is silent
j	as 'y' in 'yellow'
jie	as 'kee' in 'keep'
r	slightly rolled

s   as in 'sound'
v   as 'f' in 'feather'
w   as in 'Wagner'
y   as 'ay' in 'hay', thus *geprys* is pronounced 'gu-prace'

Argentina—see Spanish

Armenian (Armenia)

Vowels

A   as in 'arm' (long)
a   as in 'apple' (short)
e   as first 'e' in 'hence'
ee   as in 'cheese'
ə   as 'u' in 'turn'
o   as 'oi' in 'voice'
oo   as in 'boot'

Consonants

ch   as in 'cheese' (*skancheli*)
dz   as 'ds' in 'hands'
gh   a guttural rolled sound similar to a rolled 'r', except in *kaghaki* and *Betghehem*,
         where 'gh' sounds as 'ch' in 'loch'
h   as in 'hot'
j   as in 'jeep'
kh   as 'ch' in 'loch'
q   as 'si' in 'vision'
s   as in 'self'
ts   as 'tz' in 'tzar' (*orhnetsek, marmnatsav, haytnetsav*)
tz   as 'ts' but with a puff of air
y   as in 'boy'
ye   as in 'yet'

Haysm   as in 'smile'
Hovivk   as 'vehic' in 'vehicle'
Yerken   as 'Ye' in 'Yemen'
Vordik   as 'deac' in 'deacon'

Basque (Basque Country, Spain)

Vowels

All vowels are short except 'i' which is long.
a   as in 'cat'
e   as in 'get'
i   as 'ee' in 'feet'
o   as in 'hot'
u   as in 'put'

Consonants

g   as in 'good'
h   silent, thus *nahi* sounds like 'nigh'
j   as 'ch' in Scottish 'loch'
r   slightly rolled
rr   strongly rolled

tx	as 'ch' in 'chat'
tz	as 'ts' in 'bats'
x	'sh', thus *ixilean* is pronounced 'i-shi-le-an'
z	as 's'

Every syllable has equal stress. All vowels and consonants are pronounced the same in all contexts and vowel combinations are the same as the two vowels pronounced separately. For example, *gauean* is pronounced 'gow-e-an', and *artzaiari* is pronounced 'art-sigh-ya-ri'. An 'e' at the end of a word is a full vowel. For example, *ere* has two equal 'e' sounds.

Belgium—see Flemish

Brazil—see Portuguese

Canada (Quebec)—see French

Dominican Republic—see Spanish

Estonian (Estonia)

All doubled letters, whether vowels or consonants, are sounded long.

Vowels

a	as 'u' in 'truck'
ä	as in 'cat'
e	as in 'let' (closed)
i	as 'ee' in 'meet'
o	as 'a' in 'ball'
ö	as 'er' in 'term', or German 'ö' with strongly rounded lips
õ	uniquely Estonian but sounds approximately as 'oa' in 'loan'
u	as in 'boot', with strongly rounded lips
ü	as French 'u' in 'une', or German 'ü'

Consonants

p, t, k	as in English pronunciation but without aspiration
b, d, g	as weak 'p', 't', and 'k' (unvoiced)
l, m, n, v, s	as English pronunciation
r	as English 'r' but stronger
j	as 'y' in 'yet'
h	as in 'he', with strongly rounded lips

Sung consonants should all be quite strong but not over-aspirated.

Ewe (Ghana)

Vowels

a	as in 'arm' (long)
ã	nasal 'ah', like 'ya' in 'yard'
e	as 'a' in 'date'
i	as in 'hip'
o	like 'oh'
o̲	as in 'cot'
õ	nasal version of 'o' in 'cot'

oo   as in 'hoop'
u   as in German 'über'

Consonants

ɖ   a soft 'd' made with tip of tongue between the lips
ḏ   as in 'dog'
dz   as 'j' in 'just'
f   a voiceless sound produced by pursing lips and blowing
gb   a guttural elision of these two consonants
kp   as 'kip' spoken quickly
ṇ   as 'ng' in 'sing'
ny   as Spanish 'ñ'
s   as in 'sound'
ts   as 'ch' in 'chair'
x̱   as 'h' in 'hay'
y   as in 'yellow'

Finnish (Finland)

Vowels

a   as 'a' in 'father'
ä   as 'a' in 'hat'
e   as 'e' in 'set'
i   as 'i' in 'sit' (closed)
o   as 'o' in 'toy' (open)
ö   as German 'ö', or French 'eu' in 'bleue'
u   as 'oo' in 'book', but with lips more pursed
y   as German 'ü' or French 'u'

Diphthongs

ai   as 'ai' in 'aisle'
au   as 'ow' in 'cow'
äi, äy 'ä' + a short 'i' or 'y' in the same syllable
ei   as 'ey' in 'hey'
eu, iu 'e' or 'i' + a short 'u' in the same syllable
ie   as 'ie' in Spanish 'bien'
oi   as 'oi' in 'voice'
öi, öy 'ö' + a short 'i' or 'y' in the same syllable
ou   as 'o' in 'so', but more rounded
ui   as 'uy' in Spanish 'muy'
uo   as 'uo' in Italian 'buona'
yi   as 'ui' in French 'suis', but the Finnish 'y' is slightly less rounded than the French 'u'
yö   'y' + a short 'ö' in the same syllable

Consonants

g   as in 'guide'
h   as in 'hen' (audible)
j   as 'y' in 'yes'
k   as 'k' in 'pumpkin' (softer than in 'kit' and without aspiration)
l   as in 'let' (a deep sound)
ng   as in 'singing', but longer
p   as in 'spin' (softer than in 'pin' and without aspiration)

r	as Spanish 'r' (slightly rolled)
s	as in 'stop'
t	as in 'stop' (softer than in 'top' and without aspiration)

Flemish (Belgium)

Vowels

Vowels followed by a single consonant + vowel, or written double, are long; those followed by two consonants, or a final consonant, are short.

a	as in German 'das' (short) except in *tranendal*, which is pronounced 'traa-nen-dal', and *betalen*, which is pronounced 'be-taa-len'
aa	as in German 'Haar' (long)
au	as 'ou' in 'bound'
e	as 'a' in 'late' except in the first syllable of a word beginning with 'ge' or 'be', or in the last syllable, where it sounds as in 'the'. Exceptions: in *scherpe* the first 'e' sounds as in 'mac', and in *Schepper* and *Jesse* the first 'e' sounds as in 'yes'
ee	as 'a' in 'late'
ei	as 'ai' in French 'fontaine'
i	as in 'this'
ie	as 'e' in 'she'
ij	as 'ai' in French 'fontaine'
o	as in 'cot' except in *Godes*, which is pronounced 'Goo-des', and *verkoren*, which is pronounced 'ver-koo-ren'
oe	as 'o' in 'who'
oei	like 'ooy'
oo	as 'o' in 'close'
ou	as in 'bound'
u	in the first or last character of a word, as German 'ÿ' in 'blÿhen'; between other characters, as in 'shut'

Consonants

ch	as in 'Bach'
d	as in 'deer', but at the end of a word sounds 't'
g	as 'ch' in German 'ach', but slightly voiced
j	as 'y' in 'youth'
r	rolling 'r' as in 'Puerto Rico'
sch	sounds separately, as 's-ch'
w	as in German 'wir'

French (France and Quebec)

Vowels

There are no diphthongs, only pure vowels pronounced with either rounded or smiling lips.

e	at the end of a word or followed by a single consonant, sounds like 'er' but with rounded lips
é, ée, er, ez at end of word *et* (single word)	as in 'sip' but with smiling lips
ais, ait at end of word e + double consonant *ses, des, les, est* (single words)	as in 'bed' except in *faisait*, which is pronounced 'fir-zeh'
oi, oy	like 'wa'
au, eau/eaux	like 'oh', but with rounded lips

eu, eux	rather more closed than 'e' at the end of a word, with very rounded, almost closed lips
i, ie	as 'ee' in 'see'
ou	as 'oo' in 'food', with very rounded lips
u	as German 'ü', or 'ou' in 'you'

Vowels followed by 'n' or 'm' are nasalized. This consonant is not pronounced unless followed by a vowel.

ant, an, en, em, am	like 'āh' except in *Bethléem*, which is pronounced 'Bet-lay-em'
int, in, ain, ein	like 'ēh'
ont, on, om	a very closed 'õ'
um, un	as 'ũn' in English 'ũnder'
oin	as 'wēn' in English 'wēnt'

Exception: *immortel* is pronounced 'ee-mor-tel'

Consonants

All consonants are short and strong but with as little audible breath as possible.

c	as 's' (*ci, ce, ç*) or 'k' (*co, cou, ca, cu*)
ch	as 'sh'
d, t	soft, without English 'wetness'
gè	'g' is soft
gn	like 'ny' (*campagne* is pronounced 'cāh-pa-nyer')
gui	hard, like 'ghee'
h	silent
ill	as 'y' (*embrouillé* is pronounced 'āh-broo-yay')
j	soft, as 'g' in 'courgette'
qu	as 'k'
r	flipped with the tip of the tongue; never blurred as in English
s	between vowels, as 'z'
th	as 't'

Final consonants are silent except when followed by a vowel. Exceptions: in *cristal*, *l'air*, *tous*, *ouïr*, *Betléem*, *fils* (rhymes with 'police'), *il*, *retour*, *l'honneur*, and *immortel* the final consonants are sounded.

German (Germany and Switzerland)

Vowels

a	short as 'u' in 'but'; or long as in 'father' for *Amen, Maria, Vater*
e	short as in 'bed'; or long and closed as 'é' in French 'égalité' for *dem, ewige, segnet, sehn, selig, verstehn*. An 'e' in the prefix 'ge' and in an end syllable is weakly pronounced, like 'e' in 'the'
i	as in 'it' (short)
ie, ih	as 'ee' in 'fee' (long)
o	short as 'o' in 'song'; or long as in Italian 'O sole mio' for *gezogen, großer, schon*
ö	as 'or' in 'worse' (*hört*); or longer and with rounded lips as 'eu' in French 'peu'
u	short as 'oo' in 'book'; or long as 'oo' in 'boot' for *Geburt, ruht, zu*
ü	long and with very rounded lips, as 'u' in French 'tu'

Diphthongs

ai, ei	as 'y' in 'fly'
au	as 'ou' in 'loud'
äu, eu	as 'oy' in 'boy'

Consonants

ch	as 'ch' in 'loch'; or as 'ch' in 'Christian' for *Christkind*
d	as in 'dog' except when at the end of a word, when it sounds as 't' in 'bat'
h	before a vowel: pronounced; after a vowel: silent (lengthening it)
s	as 'ss' in 'miss' (unvoiced) when final, doubled, or next to a voiceless consonant; as 'z' in zebra' (voiced) when at the start of a word or syllable
ß	as 'ss' in 'miss'
sch	as 'sh' in 'shoe'
sp, st	as 'shp'/'sht' when at the start of a word or syllable
v	as 'f' in 'foam'
w	as 'v' in 'veranda'
z	as 'ts' in 'boots'

Ghana—see Ewe

Hungarian (Hungary)

Vowels

a	as 'o' in 'not' (short)
á	as 'a' in 'father' (long)
e	as in 'bed' (short)
é	as 'ea' in 'fear', but without final diphthong (long)
i	as 'i' in 'lip' (short)
í	as 'ee' in 'feed' (long)
o	as 'o' in 'sort' (short)
ó	as 'aw' in 'saw' (long)
ö	as German 'ö' or French 'eu'; similar to 'u' in 'fur' (short)
ő	a longer version of 'ö' as in German 'schön'
u	as in 'put' but more rounded (short)
ú	as 'oo' in 'boot' (long)
ü	as German 'ü' or French 'u' (short)
ű	a longer version of 'ü' above
y	as 'ee' (NB 'y' is not a vowel when it follows 'g', 'l', or 'n', when it alters the sound of the consonant)

There are no diphthongs in Hungarian; each vowel must be pronounced separately.

Consonants

c	as 'ts' in 'bats'
cs	as 'ch' in 'church' (*karácsony*)
g	hard as in 'get', unless followed by 'y'
gy	as 'dy', or 'd' in adulation (*egy*)
j	as 'y' in 'yes'. *Jaj* (the sound for a sigh) is pronounced 'y-a-y' said very quickly
ly	as 'y' in 'yes'
ny	like Spanish 'ñ', or 'ni' in 'onion' (*kinyílt*)
r	rolled but not trilled
s	as 'sh' in 'ship' (*mostan*)
sz	as 's' in 'sell' (*szép*)
ty	as first 't' in 'tutor'
z	as in 'zoo'
zs	as 's' in 'measure' (*rózsavirág*)

Double consonants are pronounced long:
dd   *hadd*
ll   *szállást*
nn   *mennyből*
ss   *lássátok*
tt   *kibimbózott*
zz   *hozzátok*

Icelandic (Iceland)

The carol text is given in Roman type, with a transcription shown below in italics.

The unvoiced 'th' sound, as in 'thin', is used at the beginning of a word; the voiced 'th' sound, as in 'than', is used in the middle or end of a word.

1. Immanúel oss í nátt
    Immanooel (soon) awss (awe) ee nowhtt (how)

    eðla barnið fæddist.
    Ethla barnith feyehdist

    Gjörir það hjartað glatt og kátt,
    Gyurir (fur) thath hyartath glatt awg (awe) kowhtt

    guðsson holdi klæddist
    Gvuthsson hawldi (awe) kleydhist (eye)

    Fyrir hann tók faðir í sátt
    Firir (fin) hahn toke fathir ee sowhtt

    fólkið allt sem mæddist.
    Folkith alt sem meyehdist (eye)

    Synd of dauði missti mátt,
    Sind awg duithi missti mowhtt

    þau mest ég áður hræddist.
    Thoy (Thui) mest yeg owthur hreyehdist (eye)

2. Vil ég mitt sálar simfóní,
    Vil yeg mitt sowlar simfoenee

    sett með bestu snilli,
    Seht meth bestu snidli

    leggja fram og leika því,
    Legya fram awg layka (day) thvee

    láta' ei stund á milli,
    Lowt ay (day) stund ow midli

    að göfga þann sem fékk oss frí,
    Ahth guvgah than sem fyek aws free

    föðurins náð og hylli;
    Futhurins nowth awg hidli

    Hljóðagóð um borg og bý
    Hlyoethagoeth (toe) um borg awg bee

    börnin Kristó dilli.
    Burnin kristoe didli.

3. Syngi þessa þakkargjörð
    Singi thessa thakkar gyurth

    því með engla kórum.
    Thvee meth engla koerum

    Heiður, lof og háleit dýrð
    Haythur lawv awg howlate deerth

    sé hæstum Guði vórum.
    Sye (yes) highstum gvuthi voerum

    Fenginn er nú fyrst á jörð
    Fenginn er (air) noo (soon) first (fist) ow (oei) yurth

    friður smám og stórum.
    Frithur smowm (how) awg stoewrum

    Faðirinn elskar auma hjörð,
    Fathirinn elskar uima hyurth

    oss sem villtir fórum.
    Awss sem vihlltir foerum.

Igbo (Nigerian)

The syllabic setting of the Nigerian carol makes pronunciation of the words relatively simple. With a few exceptions, they are pronounced exactly as they appear.

Vowels

a	as in 'hand'
e	as in 'every'
i	as 'e' in 'he'
o	as in 'old'
ọ	as in 'option'
u	as 'oo' in 'room'
ụ	as 'ou' in 'doubt'

Consonants

Nw, ny, kp, ch, gb, nn, kw: the sound is determined by the vowel that comes after them

nn	as in 'name' but with an 'n' before
nw	as in 'one' but with an 'n' before
ch	as in 'chicken'
kw	as 'ch' in 'choir'
n'i, r'a	pronounced as a single syllable
mgbe	pronounced as 'm-gbe'—'m' as in 'simple', and 'gbe' pronounced with the 'e' (as in 'engine') prominent

Irish (Ireland)

The carol text is given in Roman type, with a transcription shown below in italics.

1. Fáilte romhat a Rí na bhflaitheas,
   Foil-che roh't ah ree nuh vlah-huss

   Fáilte romhat a Aon-Mhic Dé,
   Foil-che roh't ah aeon-vik day

   A rugadh do Mhuire, máthair 'gus maighdean,
   Ah ruh-gah duh wirra, maw-hir guss my-jun

   Chun go sábhálfá sinn ón olc . . .
   Kun guh saw-wall-faw shin own ulk

   Scéala na Nollag 'nois canaimis uile:
   Shkale-uh nuh mull-ug nish konn-ah-meesh ill-uh

2. Fáilte romhat a Rí na naingeal
   Foil-che roh't ah ree nuh nang-gull

   A thánaig go teach na bpian anuas,
   Ah hawn-ig guh tyahkh nuh bee-uhn ah-noo-us

   'S a chodail i stábla bocht go humhal . . .
   suh khud-ill ih staw-bluh bukh't guh hoo-ull etc.

3. Fáilte romhat a Rí na cruinne . . .
   Foil-che roh't ah ree nuh krin-nuh

   Le háthas cuirimis guth le do ghlóir . . .
   Leh haw-huss kwir-ih-meesh guh leh doh ghlow-irr

   Ár nádúr daonna do ghlacais, a Íosa . . .
   Awr naw-duuhr day-uhn-nuh duh ghla-kish ah ee-uh-suh etc.

Korean (Korea)

Vowels

a, ah	as 'a' in 'psalm'
ae	as 'e' in 'exit'
e	as 'e' in 'them'
eh	as 'e' in 'them'
eu	as 'eu' in French 'eux'
i	as in 'sing'
o	as in 'cot'
oo	as in 'cool'
u	as 'oo' in 'cool'
uh	as 'u' in 'summer'

w + a vowel sounds as a combination of two vowels, thus *wah* is pronounced 'u-a'

Consonants

bb	a strong 'p' as in Italian 'passaggio'
ch	as in 'child'
dd	as 'th' in 'them'
g	as in 'guest'

h	as in 'hot'
j	as in 'just'
r	as in 'kyrie'
s	as in 'sound'
sh	as in 'she'

Latvian (Latvia)

Vowels

a	as in 'park' (but short)
ā	as in 'father' (longer than 'a' on its own)
e	as in 'let'
ē	as French 'er' in 'chanter'
i	as in 'bin'
ī	as 'ee' in 'meet'
u	as 'oo' in 'look'
ū	as 'oo' in 'moot'

Diphthongs

ai	as 'ai' in 'aisle'
au	as 'ow' in 'brown', or as in German 'laufen'
ie	as first 'e' in 'mere', or 'ea' in 'fear'
o	as Italian 'uo' in 'uomo' (the 'o' in *dong* is pronounced as in 'cot')

Consonants

c	as 'ts' in 'bats'
dz	as 'ds' in 'lids'
g	as in 'goat'
ņ	as French 'gn' in 'mignon'
r	rolled as in German 'Brot'
s	as in 'seven'
š	as 'sh' in 'ship'
t	as in 'lit' (slightly harder than English 't')

Nigeria—see Igbo

Norwegian (Norway)

Vowels

Vowels sound long before single consonants and short before double consonants.

a	as in 'arm' for *av* and *grann*; as 'o' in 'sock' for *sagt* and *kalde*
å	like 'awe'
ai	as 'ey' in 'eye'
e	as in 'hermit'
ei	as 'ey' in 'eye'
i	as 'ee' in 'seed' in *blid* and when alone; as 'i' in 'sing' for *midt* and *vinter*
o	as 'oo' in 'hoop' but with pursed lips, except in *som* and *om*, where 'o' sounds as in 'sock', and in *og*, where it sounds as 'oh'
u	as 'oo' in 'hoop', but with pursed lips

Consonants

d	silent except in *det*, *fedrane*, and for the first 'd' in *midnattstid*, where it sounds as in 'dog'. *Ved* with a silent 'd' sounds like 'veer' spoken quickly
g	as 'k' in 'sock' for *sagt*; as in 'guitar' for *og*

gj   as 'y' in 'yellow'
j   as 'y' in 'yellow'
ø   as 'ur' in 'hurdle'
r   slightly rolled
s   as in 'sound'
t   as in 'tall' except in *det*, where it is silent. *Det* with a silent 't' sounds like 'dear' spoken quickly

Polish (Poland)

Vowels

a   as 'u' in 'cup'
ą   a nasal 'o' as in French 'bon'. When followed by 't', ą is pronounced as oral 'o' + the nasal consonant 'n', thus *bydłątkoma* is pronounced 'by-dłon-tko-ma'
e   as in 'bed'
ę   a nasal 'e' as in French 'bien'. When followed by 't' or 'dz', ę is pronounced as oral 'e' + the nasal consonant 'n', thus *Najświętszej* is pronouced Naj-świen-tszej, *Świętego* is pronounced 'Świen-te-go', and *między* is pronounced 'mien-dzy'
i   as 'ee' in 'see'
o   as in 'pot'
ó   as 'u' in 'put'
u   as in 'put'
y   as 'y' in 'Mary'

Consonants

c   as 'ts' in 'bats'
ć   as 'c' in Italian 'ciao'
ch   as 'h' in 'hot' (also spelled 'h')
dź   as 'ć' but voiced
dz   pronounced by conflating 'd' and 'z'
dzi   like 'dź' (*porodziła*)
g   as in 'get'
h   as in 'hot'
j   as 'y' in yellow
l   as in 'leak'
ł   as 'w' in 'wet'
ń   approximately as 'ni' in 'onion'
ni   like 'ń' (*pogłowniczek*)
r   as in Italian 'ragazza'
rz   as 's' in 'measure' (also spelled 'ż')
ś   a palatal 's', as in Italian 'lasciare'
św   as 'śf', thus *Najświętszej* is pronounced 'Naj-śfien-tszej', and *Świętego* is pronounced 'Śfien-te-go'
t   as in Italian 'staccato'
w   as 'v' in 'very', but before voiceless consonants 'w' changes into 'f', thus *w co* is pronounced 'f co'; *w czym* is pronounced 'f czym'; and *w to* is pronounced 'f to'
z   as in 'zipper'
ż   as 's' in 'measure'
ź   a very soft, hissing 'z', articulated as 'ś' but voiced

Portuguese (Brazil)

Vowels

Portuguese full vowels (shown in the text with ´) are pronounced as follows:

a	as in 'cat'
e	as in 'get'
i	as 'ee' in 'feet'
o	as in 'hot'
u	as in 'put'

For example, in *Belém* the first 'e' is weak, like French 'de', but the second is full.
In *tódos* and *sómos* the first 'o' is full but the second is weak, as in 'boot'.

ais	as 'eyes'
ão	as 'ow' in 'now', but nasal. *Chão* sounds as the first syllable of 'shower', and *Dorme ao* sounds as 'meow'
ei	as 'ay' in 'day'
em, en	as 'an' in 'angel'
eu	a diphthong pronounced as the two full vowels quickly
ie	a diphthong pronounced as the two full vowels quickly (*viemos*)

Consonants

c	before 'a', 'o', or 'u', sounds as 'k'; before 'e' or 'i', sounds as 's'
ç	as 's'
ch	as 'sh'
de	at the end of a word, sounds as 'gy' in 'energy' (*verdade*)
g	before 'e' and 'i', sounds as in 'page'; before 'a', 'o', or 'u', sounds as in 'get' (*guerra*)
j	as 'si' in 'television'
lh	in the middle of a word, sounds as 'lli' in 'million'
r	at the start of a word, sounds as 'ch' in Scottish 'loch'; in the middle of a word, sounds as a slightly rolled 'r'
te	at the end of a word, sounds as 'chy' in 'starchy'

Slovenian (Slovenia)

Vowels

a	as in 'apple'
e	as in 'them'
i	as in 'bitter'
o	as in 'opera'
u	as 'oo' in 'hoop' except in *use*, when it sounds as 'woo' in 'wood'

Consonants

c	as 'ts' in 'bats'
č	as 'ch' in 'chocolate'
j	as 'y' in 'yellow'
l	as in 'leg' except in *polna*, where it sounds as 'w' in 'pow', and in *bil*, where it sounds as 'w' in 'ewe'
r	slightly rolled
s	as in 'sound'
š	as 'ch' in 'champagne'
v	as 'v' in 'villa' except *v* in line 4 of verse 4, when it is as 'oo' in 'hoop'
ž	as 'g' in 'courgette'

South Africa—see Afrikaans

Spanish (Argentina, Dominican Republic, Venezuela)

Vowels

All vowels are short except 'i' which is long.

a	as in 'cat'
e	as in 'get'
i	as 'ee' in 'feet'
o	as in 'hot'
u	as in 'put'
y	as a whole word (*y una alegre Navidad*), sounds as 'ee' in 'feet'

No vowel sounds are weak. *Arder* is pronounced 'ar-dare', with short vowels and rolled 'r' both times, and *creyente* has 3 syllables with equal 'e' sounds. Vowel combinations are pronounced the same as the two vowels separately. For example, *trae* is pronounced 'tra-e'.

Diphthongs

ai	as 'eye'
ia, ie, io, iu	'i' sounds as 'y' in 'yellow', followed by the usual vowel sound (*Dios, bien*)
ua, ue, ui, uo	'u' sounds as 'w' in 'water' (*nuestro, Pascuas*)
ey	as 'ay' in 'day' (*Rey*)

Consonants

c	as in 'car'; before an 'e' or an 'i', sounds as in 'cereal'
qui, que	as 'k' in 'keep' (*bosque*)
d	as in 'diet'; between two vowels or at the end of a word, sounds as 'th' in 'that'
b	as 'b' in 'beach'; when between two vowels sounds softer, more like an English 'v'
g	as in 'go'; before an 'i' or 'e', sounds as Scottish 'ch' in 'loch'
gue	as 'ge' in 'get' (*guerra, siguen*)
h	silent (*hermosura*)
j	as Scottish 'ch' in 'loch'
ll	as 'y' in 'yet'
ñ	as 'ni' in 'onion'
r	slightly rolled; at the beginning of a word, strongly rolled
rr	strongly rolled
z	as 's' (Central and Latin America)

Swedish (Sweden)

Vowels

a	long as in 'far' (*barn, bar, dag, svag*); or short as 'u' in 'but' (*varje, stallet, gudason, goda, natt, gamla*)
o	long as 'u' in German 'du' (*manniskobarn, manniskorna, goda, jorden, rosig, tro*); or short as in 'hot' (*och, bort, kropp, hopp*). Exception: in *gudason* the 'o' is pronounced like 'a' in 'saw'
u	long as 'ou' in 'you' (*jul, skjul, gudason, slut, nu*)
å	long as 'aw' in 'saw' (*på, bortifrån*); or short as 'o' in 'song' (*långt*)
e	long as first 'e' in here (*det, ser, ger, fred*); or short as in English 'pen' (*ett, en, varje, stallets, den, världen*)

i   long as in 'see' (*i, vi, frid, rosig*); or short as in 'did' (*till, människorna, människobarn, bortifrån, vilja*)

y   long approximately as in 'sorry' (*ny*); or short as 'ü' in German 'müssen' (*nytt, grytt*)

ä   long as the first part of 'hair' (*är, stjärnan, där, bär, värnlös*); or short as in 'carry' (*människorna, människobarn, världen*)

ö   long as 'ir' in 'bird' if followed by 'r', otherwise similar to 'eu' in French 'deux' (*föds, gör*); short is similar but with a shorter pronounciation (*fött*)

Consonants

ch   in *och* is pronounced 'k'

g   as in 'good' when before 'a', 'o', 'u', 'å', consonants, and at the end of words (*gudason, dag, grytt, goda, rosig*); as 'y' in 'yes' when before 'e', 'i', 'y', 'ä', 'ö', and after 'l' and 'r' (*gör, ger*)

j   as 'y' in 'yes' (*jul, varje, viljan, jorden*)

sk(j) as 'sh' in 'shall' (*människobarn, människorna, skjul*)

stj   as 'sh' in 'shall' (*stjärna*)

Silent consonants

t   silent in *det*

r   soft and rolling when at the end of a word or in front of a vowel. If in front of a consonant it is almost silent, as in 'hard' (*jorden*). Exception: in *varje* 'r' is pronounced as a soft rolling r

l   silent in *världen*

Switzerland—see German

Venezuela—see Spanish